THE
MONEY MAP
METHOD

LIFELONG WEALTH
IN A FOREVER-CHANGED WORLD

Keith Fitz-Gerald

Money Map Press • Baltimore, Maryland

THE
M●NEY MAP
PRESS

The advice and strategies in this book constitute the opinions of the author and may not be appropriate for your personal financial situation. You should therefore seek the advice and services of a competent financial professional before utilizing any of the investment strategies advocated in this book.

www.moneymappress.com

Table of Contents

Chapter Two (Continued...)

Chapter Three: Putting the Method into Action

Chapter Four: Key Questions

Appendix One: Says Who?

Appendix Two: Money Map Building Blocks

About the Author

Introduction

Once Upon a Time...

...Investing was fairly simple. You identified a company in the United States with solid management, a good product, rapidly growing sales, a storehouse of cash, and competitive advantages... and you bought that company's stock and sat back to wait.

Keith Fitz-Gerald

Chief Investment Strategist

Money Map Press

With just a little bit of luck and a growing economy, it rose in price, giving you a profit for your efforts.

To quote Archie Bunker, "Those were the days..."

But those days are gone – and they are not coming back.

Today, companies with the highest-flying returns operate all around the globe. And thanks to unprecedented central bank meddling, trillions in derivatives, a complete loss of faith in Washington, global electronic markets, and high-frequency trading systems, years of buy-and-hold gains can be wiped out in seconds.

So, what's an individual investor to do? Can you still compete in today's new financial world?

Yes, you can. You just need a system.

Welcome to the Money Map Method!

On the pages that follow, you will discover a simple, no-nonsense approach to saving more, investing better, and building mega wealth in the years ahead.

You'll learn:

▶ Why things will never return to the way they were...

- ▶ What the coming decades of deleveraging means for your money and investments...

- ▶ And most importantly, how to capitalize on the opportunities being created right now.

I'm talking about specific steps you can take to build real wealth for the years ahead, even if you only have a few years until retirement, or you just want to get the maximum work out of your money.

Before we get started, whenever I talk about the Money Map Method, I get lots of questions. Let's answer the key ones right up front, so you can decide if this book is for you:

Q: Why do I need the Money Map Method?

A: It's a tough world out there for investors. And it's only getting tougher.

Yields are being held artificially low by central bankers and policy wonks who don't understand how real money works. Wall Street is doing everything it can to resist regulations that would rein it in and make things safer for the "everyday" investor – because they might crimp profits for the banksters.

Meanwhile, our leaders can't be bothered by the very real need to help millions of citizens caught in the eye of a financial vortex. Instead, they're focused on more bailouts, their own re-election campaigns, and building a "handout society." No wonder confidence in our leaders is in short supply...

We are now in an era of zero interest rates, negligible growth, unprecedented government meddling, continuous deleveraging, and a historic level of debt. Investors need to know what the world really looks like and why... how to spot high-probability opportunities... and ways to earn not just appreciation, but also income from their investments.

If you want to achieve your financial dreams, you've got to take matters into your *own* hands.

That's what the Money Map Method is for.

Q: How has the approach to investing changed in the past 20 years?

A: People have finally come to understand that too much debt is a bad thing.

It's bad for investors. It's bad for companies. And it's bad for entire countries. The United States is no exception. You simply cannot spend more money than you have and expect exponential growth to continue forever.

Investors have also learned the hard way, in 2000, again in 2007, and, indeed, since the current financial crisis started, that Wall Street's highly touted "diversification" model is little more than a sales pitch. *Diversification doesn't work.* Spreading your money out to get the lowest mean gains is not a recipe for wealth. The best professional investors of our time DO NOT blindly distribute their money across a slew of asset classes, and individual investors should not do it either.

We also know that long-held assumptions surrounding the roles of growth and income are no longer true.

For example, people like to believe the rapid growth of the 1990s is normal, and we're now dragging. Yet history shows that growth at those rates is an anomaly. You cannot routinely invest in stocks and expect them to automatically go up forever – a strategy I call "buy and hope." "Buy and manage" is a much more appropriate way to do things.

We've also discovered more about the role of unregulated financial instruments and the dangers associated with high-speed trading. An estimated 70% of all stock trading activity is now computer-driven – and unless you are using specific strategies to defend against that, sooner or later you and your money will be separated.

Finally, there is no longer any doubt about the incestuous relationship between Wall Street, its "regulators," and Washington. Insiders continue to run the show. Individual investors must take steps to mitigate the risk of further malfeasance, or they will almost certainly be taken on another white-knuckle ride they didn't sign up for.

But don't completely forsake the markets. Not everything is doom and gloom. Quite the opposite.

As the world struggles with the ongoing financial crisis, newly emerging markets in the United States and abroad are transforming the future for those investors who see what's coming. That's very exciting, even though it's not without its own challenges for the United States, Europe, and Japan – all of which have historically dominated the investing landscape.

There are so many changes going on in the financial world. Unless you truly understand them, and know what to do, you'll have little chance of doing well over the long run.

Q: What issues concern investors the most right now?

A: Many investors are in dire financial straits today, after the 2008 financial crisis slashed their assets by 50% (on average).

Retirement looks further away than ever.

To catch up, they need to achieve steady, oversized gains to reach their goals. But they can't incur unnecessary risk. They don't want to chase the current craze or be taken in by hype that just ends up in losses that could decimate their portfolios.

Q: What's the most important thing an investor can do today, as we bounce from one crisis to another?

A: I believe the 50-40-10 Strategy you'll see in Chapter Two and safety-first investment choices are the strongest foundation for growth. Not coincidentally, both are also the best defense against the next financial calamity.

To that end, I recommend the Money Map Method because it relies on careful study, well-reasoned choices and an emphasis on high income and safety-first stability.

Home runs are nice – and the Money Map Method does produce many triple-digit gains. But in this day and age, *consistency* and *certainty* are more important when it comes to building a nest egg of $1 million – the average dollar figure needed for a decent retirement. These are all topics addressed in the Money Map Method.

Q: Is this book for me?

A: I sure hope so. The information it holds will help you grow and maintain the money that you, your children, and your family may need in the years to come.

In fact, the way I see things, learning these secrets of the Money Map Method is no longer optional.

It doesn't matter whether you manage your own money or have somebody do it for you. You can no longer confine your investing activity to strategies that worked in the 1980s or 1990s.

Many of those concepts have been made moot by a colossal shift of social, political, and economic power. That same "shift" is creating immediate and unprecedented opportunities for individuals who want to secure the safe, consistent, and strong gains they need, as well as some huge grand slams along the way.

If you're tempted to dismiss this information, do so at your own risk.

More than three billion people will join the global economic "conversation" within the next 10 years. Their involvement will fuel entirely new connections between products, services, and specific investment opportunities that few have even begun to contemplate.

Ironically, our political leaders and central bankers will do everything in their power to block this shift. But they will not succeed. I believe they have reached the limits of their crony capitalism, bailouts, and unchallenged exercise of their power.

In place of those ineffective actions, we will see solutions based on economic growth, pure capitalism, and the power of billions of people who simply want to enjoy a higher standard of living.

We will also witness an unprecedented shift into non-dollar, non-euro currencies. This is going to rewrite the laws of finance, politics, social development, and, most importantly, *investing*.

Huge amounts of money will be made – and lost – in the continuing transition.

It's really all about your future and the opportunities you will have to allow your money to provide for you into the future.

That's my goal in writing the Money Map Method – to deliver a message that I hope all investors will understand... and profit from.

Key Takeaway:

Investors who tried to match the S&P 500 since August 2000 could have eked out 14.62% over the past 13 years. That contrasts sharply with the 287.54% return an investor using the Money Map Method's 50-40-10 strategy could have achieved with simple annual rebalancing over the same timeframe. (You'll see exactly how this strategy works – and why it's so powerful – in Chapter Two.)

Looking ahead, I believe the Money Map Method will continue to demonstrate similar outperformance, especially as financial conditions become more complicated and the markets more volatile.

The Money Map Advantage

The reasonable man adapts himself to the world; the unreasonable one persists in trying to adapt the world to himself. Therefore all progress depends on the unreasonable man.

– George Bernard Shaw, *Maxims for Revolutionists*

The biggest challenge facing investors today is a complete lack of confidence in our financial markets, our bankers, regulators, and, of course, our political leaders.

Until recently, investors were willing to ignore such things, blithely pushing the markets to record highs in late 1999 and in 2007. Now, in 2013, they've done it again.

Leading up to the 2007 financial crisis, in particular, too many investors turned a blind eye to market fundamentals like debt and a negative savings rate – measurements that would normally broadcast massive "red flags" of warning.

They forgot about concepts like value and real growth – the only true indicators of wealth creation. Instead they focused on fancy-pants financial engineering that produced the *illusion* of profitability.

Then, when the markets turned, all hell broke loose.

Negative news became self-defeating and, even worse, self-reinforcing. Legions of investors lost their shirts and sold in panic for the second time in less than a decade. It was an orgy of bailouts, shakeouts, and washouts that saw the Dow Jones Industrials lose 52.8% of their value from September 2008 to March 2009. The U.S. markets alone erased $9.3 trillion in shareholder wealth – $1.4 trillion of that in a single day (September 29, 2008).

In the wake of that chaos, many investors remain trapped on the sidelines, paralyzed like a deer in the headlights. Some are waiting for the "all clear" or for "things to improve" before they move back into the markets. Others have sworn they'll never own another stock as long as they live.

Such thinking may feel good, but it could cost you your financial future.

The solution is not to abandon the world of investing, but rather to recognize that it's a different world today – with a totally different set of rules. That's where the Money Map Method comes in.

Play by the old rules and you lose. Understand the new rules and you can win the game.

The Financial World Has All New Rules

Here are the three "new rules" you need to know to succeed as an investor today:

1. **Bailouts are a fallacy.** In all of recorded history, bailouts have never worked on anything other than an extremely short-term basis. And over time, they actually make things worse.

   Whether through interest-rate manipulation, currency devaluation, or direct cash payments, short-term infusions of money by governments *cannot* create long-term value. In fact, they opposite is true. Over time, government bailouts cannibalize wealth and stifle growth rather than fostering it.

2. **A rising tide does not lift all boats.** Despite tremendous stock market runs, the United States, Europe, and Japan are still struggling. All three are likely to be hobbled by legacy debt for decades. But make no mistake about it: The *global* economy is still growing – fueled by three billion people eager to improve their standards of living and willing to spend the trillions of dollars needed to do it.

   No doubt these up-and-comers will continue to lag behind the citizens of "developed" nations, in terms of individual economic status, for years to come. But the growth trends are unstoppable – and they're picking up speed. More than any other factor, this is what's creating the greatest opportunities for investors.

Already, the capitalization of companies in markets serving these emerging populations is growing at a rate three to five times faster than in developed nations, even though their share of overall market value is barely 1/10th of global totals.

3. **Money is still a zero-sum game.** Individual investors may have trouble recognizing opportunity – but money doesn't.

Money always moves from one bubble to the next. But it doesn't chase growth. That's a commonly held misconception. Rather, it goes where it can enjoy the greatest leverage, and it's that *leverage* that produces growth. The more leverage, the greater the growth.

Unfortunately, we're not going to get any more leverage any time soon. In fact, we're going to be busy "deleveraging" for years to come. That will suck money out of the system. Sure, the central bankers will pump in more cash in a desperate attempt to prop up the system. But the laws of money are immutable.

Eventually the system will bleed out its excess. We don't know precisely when that's going to happen – nor do we especially care – but we are acutely aware that we need a new investment method capable of keeping us in the game while defending us against the downside of an extended deleveraging.

Keeping those three rules in mind, let's talk a little more about what's really going on in today's world – and what you can do to conquer the new and unique situations we face.

Then, with that as a foundation, we'll jump into the really fun stuff... like how you can utilize the Money Map Method to earn your way to the financial future you want.

And finally, we'll follow up with specific thoughts on how to deal with various types of investments in today's new financial world.

Onward!

It's Not a Recovery, It's a "Slowcovery"

The classic economic cycle has just four basic phases:

1. **Expansion (boom)**
2. **Slowdown (bust)**
3. **Recession**
4. **Recovery**

This time around, the boom and the bust were easily identifiable. The recession, however, has teetered between single-dip and double-dip, with some declaring it a full-blown depression.

What we aren't seeing yet is a clear and sustained recovery – and, in my opinion, *we won't*.

And let's be clear... just because the S&P 500 is flirting with new all-time highs as of this writing, that doesn't mean we're in a recovery. All it does mean is that the Fed is still propping up the economy.

Instead, we're experiencing what I call a "slowcovery," or a "barbeque economy."

There are all sorts of numbers I could cite in support of that assessment, but you need to look no further than recent U.S. employment.

The Problem with "The Smartest Guys in the Room"

Why do guys like Ben Bernanke, Paul Krugman, our Congress, the European Central Bank, and nearly every leader in the EU (except Germany Chancellor Angela Merkel) still like the idea of printing their way out of this mess?

Three reasons:

- They want to get re-elected and/or maintain their own power base, in a dramatic demonstration of Parkinson's Law. (The law goes something like this: "Work expands so as to fill the time available for its completion.")

- They have failed to understand the lessons from Japan's experience (and 2,000 years of recorded monetary history before that).

- They cannot comprehend that this crisis was caused by too much money, rather than too little. Therefore, they won't admit what they are doing isn't working or think of pursuing another course of action.

Many pundits claim that the unemployment numbers are improving.

They are – if you don't look at what we've lost to begin with. And how many people have given up working and left the work force.

As of this writing, unemployment stands at 7.7%. That's not counting the 9.2% who are underemployed or who have given up looking for work. Factor them in, and the true overall figure is 14.4%. If you look at the problem a different way, participation in the civilian labor force by those able to work actually dropped 0.2% in the last reporting period – to just 63.6%.

Despite modest improvement in 2012, America still has 5.2 million fewer non-farm jobs than it did in 2007.

That's hardly a recovery.

And quantitative easing (stimulus, money-printing, whatever you call it) is not creating jobs, despite the government's claims.

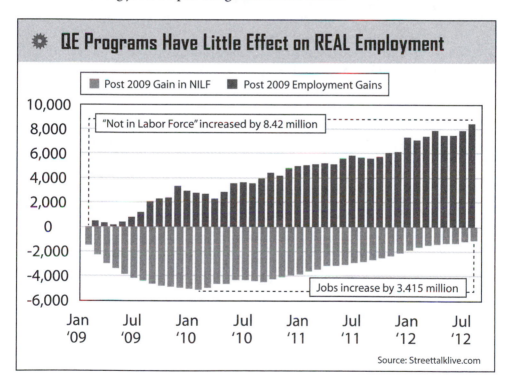

QE Programs Have Little Effect on REAL Employment

Legend: Post 2009 Gain in NILF | Post 2009 Employment Gains

"Not in Labor Force" increased by 8.42 million

Jobs increase by 3.415 million

Source: Streettalklive.com

The "Real" U.S. Federal Deficit

Also dragging heavily on any hopes for recovery is the issue of debt. Given the state of the general economy, corporate earnings reports have been surprisingly good for a while now. But, if you look closely at the numbers, you'll see that it was companies with lots of cash – not lots of debt – that performed well. You'll also see that earnings are slowing.

Now, with rates beginning to creep up, many companies are going to find out the hard way that servicing that debt leaves very little fuel for growth.

Sadly, that's a lesson in fundamental economics that our leaders in state and federal governments refuse to recognize.

Unlike you and I, who save and invest for our futures, our politicians spend and borrow for it.

Instead of stockpiling money when things are good, our re-election-hungry leaders hand out cash like candy, frolicking about in a repetitive orgy of spending... and borrowing... and more spending...

Now, five years after the "bust" – five years of slow or no growth, plummeting tax receipts, and heavier demand for benefits and bailouts – they can't understand why they're strapped for cash.

What's worse, they think more of the same will solve the problem, blithely believing they'll be able to squeeze more blood out of a desiccated turnip.

No doubt, the Fiscal Cliff issues got lots of media attention and lip service, but all we got at the end of the day was a Band-Aid-like fix, higher taxes, and no meaningful solutions.

All the talk of a $15 trillion or $16 trillion federal deficit is based on "fudged" numbers to justify billions in added benefits for Medicaid, Medicare, and "ObamaCare," as well as trillions in future liabilities under Social Security. In truth, we owe ourselves $222 trillion. No, I'm not pulling that number out of thin air... (See the sidebar on the next page for details).

With that kind of burden hanging over our heads, a "slowcovery" is actually a gift. We could very easily fall into a "no-covery!"

Why Exponential Growth Is Never Sustainable

Another reason political leaders (and many investors) get into financial trouble is that they believe every new period of recovery and ensuing economic expansion will last forever.

It won't.

Simply put, exponential economic growth is never sustainable.

The politicians and central bankers who think they can foster ever-increasing growth through spending, bailouts, and monetary manipulations are really just perpetrating a massive "pyramid scheme."

Traditional pyramid schemes involve some sort of crooked operation that survives off a constant influx of people investing their money. The people at the top of the pyramid get paid for a while, but you need exponential growth in the number of new investors to keep the pyramid standing. When too many people start wanting their money back, the pyramid collapses.

As sinister as that is on a limited scale, it's even more troubling when applied to an entire economic system. The end result is pre-determined:

<u>Debt-fed economic pyramids always collapse.</u>

The only unknown is how much longer the present one stays standing before it, too, comes tumbling down.

Much Ado About (Almost) Nothing

They get a lot of media attention and scare investors and markets. But Congressional budget fights are really just a sideshow.

To see what I mean, remember the debt ceiling "crisis" of 2011 – and the ongoing "fiscal cliff" drama at the end of 2012? Our leaders were fighting over the additional $2.1 trillion we've spent since the last embarrassing budget-ceiling debate, when that's really just small change.

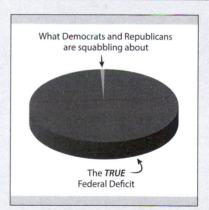

What Democrats and Republicans are squabbling about

The *TRUE* Federal Deficit

Meanwhile, America's actual "fiscal gap" – the present-value difference between projected spending and future income – is a staggering $222 trillion. That represents the true federal deficit, based on recent Congressional Budget Office data analyzed by Laurence Kotlikoff in a special study for the National Center for Policy Analysis. And it's growing fast, $11 trillion higher at press time than it was the year before.

Sadly, the politicians and bankers couldn't care less... as long as it lasts through the next election cycle and the collapse happens on the next guy's watch.

As investors, we must adopt a different perspective based on reality. America's economic pyramid has been building for a much longer time – and at an obviously unsustainable rate of growth.

As the chart below shows, U.S. gross domestic product (GDP) has been repeatedly doubling and doubling in an exponential curve for the last 60 years!

It's no wonder that the rate of growth is slowing. Nothing goes up forever and nothing grows this fast for this long – except cancer.

When will it completely reverse and collapse? That's anybody's guess. We've already seen a warning break in the curve in 2007 and 2008, and the next downturn could be even sharper.

That's why you've simply got to adopt a new way of doing things – to avoid getting clobbered when it ultimately gets here (and to profit in the meantime).

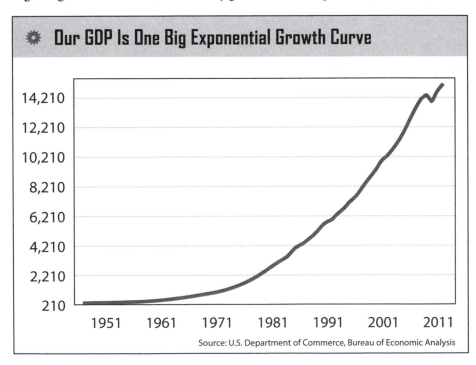

Our GDP Is One Big Exponential Growth Curve

Source: U.S. Department of Commerce, Bureau of Economic Analysis

Today's Investment "World" Spans the Globe

Part of the new approach underlying the Money Map Method is the recognition that today's investment world is much larger than the West – or even the United States, Europe, and Japan, which have collectively dominated the global economy in the second half of the 20th century.

There are investments around the world that deserve our attention.

You've also got to acknowledge that the current crisis is by no means the end of opportunity.

I know it's hard to look at the headlines and truly believe that. After all, what do you see?

Sovereign-debt dilemmas in the Eurozone... failing fiscal experiments on both sides of the pond... wild swings in investor sentiment... Facebook's botched IPO... a fresh set of White House scandals, still more concentrated financial sector risk...

It's a long and singularly disturbing list.

Even China, the brightest spot of the past decade, has gotten into the act. Renewed fears that nation is slowing lend credence to fears that the world's entire economy is heading back into the tank.

However, before you succumb to those fears, consider the following:

Full-scale global recessions are actually very rare.

In the last 40 years, there has been only one year in which the world's entire economy registered a recession – and that was in 2009, when the global economy shrank by 2.33% in the wake of the international financial crisis.

There have, of course, been global *slowdowns*. Indeed, since 1971, global GDP has slowed to an annual rate of 2.0% or less on 10 occasions.

Now, if you adhere to classic economic theory, that's a bad thing. You sure don't want to be buying stocks when global GDP growth has dipped below 2.0%... Right?

Wrong! Throw theory aside and look at the data. You'll see just as easily as I do that such slow-growth years were actually the best buying opportunities of the past 40 years.

In the 24 months following each of the years when annual GDP growth was 2.0% or less, the S&P 500 returned an average of 20.15%. That's more than double the S&P's 9.22% average return in the 24-month periods following each of the years when global GDP growth blossomed to 4.5% or better.

Those numbers probably run counter to what you've always thought – but they shouldn't. Especially if you adopt a global perspective, rather than simply looking over the fence from your own backyard.

Change Your Perspective, and It Makes Sense

When global economic activity slows down, central bankers around the world are more likely to be accommodative. That is, they loosen up the "purse strings" on money. And markets positively love easy money. Everybody knows it's a recipe for disaster, but, like an addict seeking a quick fix, the lure is irresistible. That's because lower interest rates in the wake of slower GDP growth pulls money from bonds into stocks, and stocks rally.

By contrast, when global economic activity begins to run too hot, central bankers tend to put on the brakes. They tighten monetary policy – and stock markets are less thrilled with that.

So here's the lesson...

Embrace chaos and question euphoria. Invest when sentiment is gloomy... and be wary when the masses think everything is rosy.

If everyone around you suggests you're crazy for doing that, just remember these immortal words of economist and value investor Benjamin Graham:

"You are not right because people agree with you. You are right because your facts are right, and your reasoning is right. Stick with your reasoning and don't be led astray by Wall Street's fashions and illusions."

So, where are we today? What are the "right" facts?

Here's What You Need to Know to Invest Today

The Organization for Economic Co-operation and Development (OECD) recently slashed global growth estimates to a mere 2%, as leaders in the United States, Europe, and Japan have failed yet again to deliver anything remotely resembling comprehensive debt solutions, instead electing to spend still more money!

That's well below the world's average annual GDP growth of 3.2% from 1971 to 2010.

This adjustment shouldn't come as a huge shock.

The high priests of finance bill spending as necessary to shed risk; in fact, they are using it to take risk to an entirely new and unprecedented level. The hope is that somehow this will eventually ignite growth to the point where shoddy debt can be transferred back to the markets and lower the costs associated with growth.

The way I see it, the entire world has been e-CONned. The use of debt is so far above what the markets actually require that these are purely speculative actions. But that's a story for another time...

What you need to come to terms with now is that the economic situation is still fragile, which is why Fed Chairman Bernanke continues to stick to the plan... and is determined to keep rates low at least until 2015.

Again, in theory, this is good for the economy. It allows U.S. companies to borrow new capital or refinance existing debt at some of the lowest rates in history. It also inspires (or almost forces) key central banks around the world to loosen monetary policy and keep rates low, which puts fresh wind in the sails of what I call "glocal" companies (global + local – companies that operate in multiple nations around the world).

In reality, however, it's absolutely the wrong thing to do.

By propping up functionally insolvent institutions and throwing good money after bad, Bernanke is engineering the mother of all financial catastrophes, albeit one that's down the road. His view is that failure is bad.

Unfortunately, history doesn't bear this out. In fact, the past is littered with the bones of dead financial institutions. This crisis shouldn't be any different.

Yet it is... simply because the markets are addicted to cheap money. They're running higher on the mere probability of growth instead of actual growth.

This creates a real paradox. Regardless of whether you agree with me and think stimulus is a bad idea because it delays the inevitable, or whether you disagree with me and think it's necessary, you have to go along for the ride... or risk being left so far behind you'll never catch up.

The old adage "don't fight the Fed" is very true. Only now it's "don't fight the Feds" – as in plural.

As of press time, Bernanke is no longer alone. His counterparts at the ECB and Bank of Japan are on board the cheap money express, too.

The Bears Disagree – But Don't Let That Confuse You

If you listen to the arguments of current market bears, you'd think that the "probability" of growth was actually an "impossibility."

They argue that the economy continues to drag, despite persistent monetary easing and, now that the Fed is essentially out of bullets, it has little firepower left to keep the United States from sliding back into recession, with the rest of the world close behind.

They cite money flows in the billions that have left stock funds and not returned.

They harp on the disconnect between earnings and actual economic conditions. They fear for collapse because each successive intervention seems to have less effect than the one before it.

They talk about negative real yields and capital weakness.

And they note that there have been just three significant market corrections in more than 50 months with nothing even remotely resembling a substantial decline since the beginning of the year.

The markets "must" fall, they reason.

I can't argue with anything they say... I agree.

However...

Once Again, Bad News Is Probably Good

Stocks have not looked this cheap relative to bonds in more than 50 years – a point often noted by market bulls. They contend that stocks are cheap – not because they lack value, but rather because the bears have taken control with little regard for anything other than doom and gloom headlines, fear, and market timing.

And, as with the historical growth numbers cited earlier, this apparently bad news is probably good.

That's because excessive negative sentiment toward equities – as demonstrated by the flight to bonds – typically foreshadows a positive stock market response.

In fact, according to Bespoke Investment Group, when the American Association of Individual Investors' (AAII) Bullish Sentiment Index dips below 25%, as it did in May 2012 and again in April 2013, the S&P 500 sees positive returns 86.24% of the time, with respective gains of 5.3% and 9.6% over the next three to six months.

I believe we are, in fact, almost through the worst of the global slowdown. But we could experience one more leg down before the markets stage another multi-decade secular bull run to the upside.

That's actually supported not just by emotion, but by an analysis of recent market valuations.

As of the close on Friday, November 2, 2012, the S&P 500 stood at 1,414.20, with a projected price/earnings ratio (PE) of 13.65 for the 12 months going forward, based on forecasted profits of $103.58. If the market is to come back in line with historical norms, as this next chart shows it repeatedly has since 1871, one of two things will have to happen:

1. If prices stay the same for the next 12 months, earnings will have to fall 16.75% – to approximately $86.23 per share – to bring the S&P 500's PE ratio back into line with its 50-year average of 16.4; or,

2. If earnings are held constant over the next year, the S&P 500 will have to rise a staggering 284 points, or 20.11%, to roughly 1,698.70 to reach the same 16.4 average PE multiple.

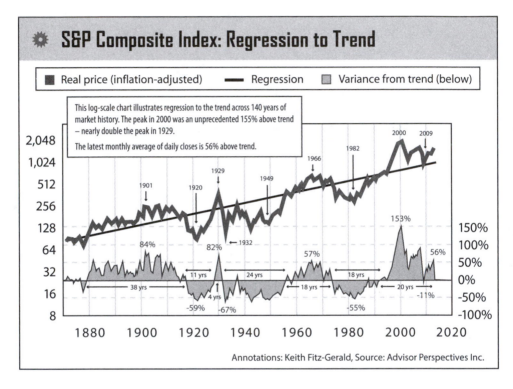

From my perspective, I think we are much more likely to see Scenario No. 1 – declining earnings – rather than rising prices. That's simply because I don't believe the sluggish economy can support the positive results reported by many companies in Q2 and Q3/2012, as evidenced by the number of firms that also lowered their future earnings outlooks.

Those reduced estimates were generally received negatively. But such a drop in expectations is actually a good thing. That's because the biggest rallies – and I'm talking about generational buying opportunities here – have historically started when PE ratios dropped into the single digits.

However, before such buying opportunities can occur – marking the start of a period of long-term economic growth and spectacular investor returns – the market has to capitulate with a sense of doom and gloom. That's what the slowing economies in the United States, Europe, and China, as well as the flight to bonds, is setting up.

As such, rather than joining the crowd in fear and worry, I believe right now is actually the time to focus on a "buy list" of solid companies that could soon be put on sale by emotionally charged investors.

In the words of legendary investor Sir John Templeton, "The time of maximum pessimism is the best time to buy."

Lord Rothschild is reputed to have been even more blunt, saying, "The best time to buy is when there's blood in the streets."

I'll add to that – "Even if it's ours."

Given that assessment, how do you actually identify the "solid companies" you should start putting on your buy list?

The Immutable Value of Growth

Earlier, I talked about the unsustainable nature of exponential growth at the systemic level. Exponential systemic growth is, without question, a bad thing, since it always leads to a collapse.

However, there's a huge difference between exponential systemic growth and *steady growth by specific companies* – both in terms of sustainability and in the returns they provide for investors.

The Real Multiplier Effect

A multiplier effect is the result of one person's spending becoming another's income... and the effect it has on subsequent transactions over time. With its roots firmly in Keynesian economics, the government believes that every $1 it spends produces between $1 and $4 in economic activity.

In reality, consumer and business spending actually decreases after government spending. Further, the government multiple is probably closer to 0.8, as suggested by Harvard economics professor Robert Barro. That means for every $1 the government spends, it generates about $0.80. Oops.

If the government's wildest multiplier dreams were true, our economy would be screaming along at 3%-4% growth and we'd have less than 4% unemployment, having spent trillions in simulative funds. But we don't.

Government spending merely redistributes wealth from the private sector, while robbing it of critical momentum. That's why the tax-the-rich argument is so badly flawed. Taxes do nothing more than involuntarily transfer wealth from consumer to government, while displacing spending and investment.

Indeed, regardless of what Bernanke and his banking cronies around the world might believe, it is only through steady and sustained growth that corporations create value – value that attracts money and leads to rising prices for both individual stocks and markets as a whole.

Specifically, value is created when three things happen:

1. **Consumerism, hope, and confidence increase.**

2. **Gains in corporate revenues and earnings reflect innovation and top-line sales growth** rather than just improved efficiency.

3. **Rising demand for products, goods, and services** makes the stock of the companies producing them worth more

Over time, these events create a true "multiplier" effect. It is fed by the increasing number of people who want a part of the action and who not only consume, but create new companies as well.

Those companies eventually become publicly traded. And as the number of listings on any exchange goes up, it increases the overall market capitalization of the respective nation or nations where the new shares are traded.

That's one of the key elements the Money Map Method takes into account when laying out strategies for investing in the new world to come.

Now, if you want to buy maximum growth, you'll have to realize one thing...

"Other" Nations Are Marching Forward at a Rapid Rate

That's because markets like the United States, Europe, and Japan are mature, and the percentage of new stock listings as a function of capitalization and GDP is now relatively small.

On the other hand, markets like those in China, much of South America, Africa, and the Middle East remain comparatively small and undercapitalized. Many are still dominated by state-owned companies.

As a result, these nations are hotbeds of potential upside.

This is particularly true for countries like those making up the CIVETS, the N-11 or the MIKTs, where the governments, their citizens and their companies are in transition.

These markets, much to the disbelief of the globe's developed countries, are increasingly independent of the "modern nations," giving them an unprecedented range of development options for the first time in history.

To fully capitalize on these options, and draw even more foreign investments, some of these countries – China, Malaysia, and Vietnam, to name three – are pouring vast sums of money into new technology. They want to modernize the stock and commodity exchanges that will carry their economic value to the world.

It's also why these same countries – once notorious for corruption, graft, and insider dealing – are transforming their legal systems in ways that Westerners will both recognize and understand. Examples include standardized settlement systems, closely regulated clearing operations, and a transparent trading infrastructure.

Don't be confused: I'm not saying all underdeveloped markets are becoming "Western." But they are beginning to use tools, structures, and systems Westerners recognize as essential to wealth creation.

> **Global Glossary:**
>
> **BRICS** – An association of large, fast-growing emerging economies Brazil, Russia, India, China, and South Africa that has held annual summits since 2009.
>
> **CIVETS** – A bloc of developing nations composed of Colombia, Indonesia, Vietnam, Egypt, Turkey and, by some definitions, South Africa, though that country is now most often included among the BRICS.
>
> **N-11** – Short for the "Next Eleven," this is an economic block of nations, in some cases overlapping the BRICS and CIVETS, made up of Bangladesh, Egypt, Indonesia, Iran, Mexico, Nigeria, Pakistan, the Philippines, Turkey, South Korea, and Vietnam.
>
> **MIKTs** – Another economic bloc consisting of Mexico, Indonesia, Korea, and Turkey.

...And Asia Is Rising – Again

Of course, you can't talk about future wealth creation – or even a potential global economic recovery – without noting the elephant in the room. Or, more accurately, the dragon.

China.

The fact is, money is steadily fleeing the "nanny states" of the West and taking up residence in the faster-growing economies of the East, led by China.

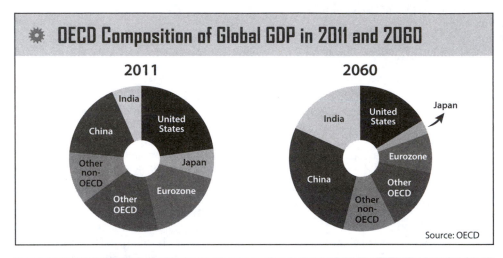

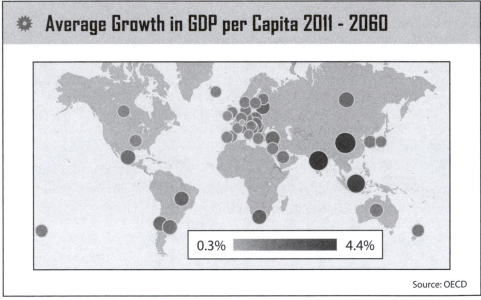

This is simply a matter of numbers.

Three of every five people alive today live in Asia. The middle class in China alone is fast approaching 600 million people – or nearly double the population of the entire United States. That's up from just 100 million in 2003... and the concept of a "middle class" didn't even exist in China in 1970.

Throw in India, and you're talking another 250 million or so, for a total of 850 million people – roughly 12.1% of the world's total population of just over seven billion – in just two Asian nations. And those numbers are expected to double by 2025!

There's simply no turning back.

There are already more than a billion new "economically empowered people" in the world. And they all want washers, dryers, TVs, stereos, computers, and cars.

And that doesn't even factor in the estimated 2.6 billion people (37% of the world population) who still live on less than $2 per day, but want more – and will probably get it. Give these people just one extra dollar per day, and you're talking about another $950 billion in annual purchasing power!

In short, the genie is not going back in the bottle – ever.

Key Takeaway:

Contrary to what many people believe, emerging market consumers are no different than you and I. We all want the same creature comforts and a higher standard of living.

But the distinction can be drawn when it comes to disposable income. By developed standards, they have very little, whereas we have a lot. That's why companies catering to the dynamic demand of rising income make tremendous sense as investments.

For example, I have my eye on a $744-million chipmaker that specializes in making system-on-a-chip chipsets for white-label phones built specifically for emerging market consumers. With approximately 500 million people in Asia moving into their own version of middle class by 2025, and still more in Africa and the Middle East, I think this company could have decades of profits ahead of it. I'll let you know when we're ready to move on it.

China is now set to overtake the United States as the world's largest economy within the next five years. India will overtake Japan within the next decade.

By 2060, at the very latest, China's and India's combined GDP will be larger than all 34 developed countries that make up the OECD put together.

In plain terms, this means that the unweighted average growth in non-OECD countries will be 3.0% per year while OECD countries will tack on growth of only 1.7% annually.

In practical terms, the per-capita GDP growth rates of the poorest countries will more than quadruple. China and India will experience a seven-fold growth in per capita GDP.

That stands in stark contrast to the United States and the European Union, which will limp along for years.

China's potential merits special attention because strong productivity and rising capital intensity will take China's per-capita income 25% above current U.S. levels. Again, that's according to the OECD.

Key Takeaway:

Consumer spending habits change markedly as per-capita income increases. Nowhere is this more evident than in China, where purchasing has shifted from essentials to discretionary, up-market items and the manufacturing that has to be built to fuel it all.

Right now I'm watching a U.S.-based company that provides global manufacturing solutions very closely because I expect the 20% of its revenue presently derived from Chinese exposure to double in the next five years and take earnings to new highs over the same time frame. Again, stay tuned for details.

Asia's ever-increasing economic potential is already attracting the world's "super-rich." They recognize that it will be far easier to create new wealth there in the coming years than anywhere else around the globe.

For example, in 2007, the legendary Jim Rogers gave up New York and landed in Singapore, where, he says, he's "preparing his daughters for the 21st century." By that, he means they understand the Asian culture, and they speak perfect Mandarin.

Facebook co-founder Eduardo Saverin, who appears on *Forbes'* list of global billionaires, recently followed suit, moving to Singapore in 2012. He even went so far as to renounce his U.S. citizenship to avoid heavy taxes.

Rogers recently told CNN, "It's easier to get rich in Asia than it is in America now" – and I don't disagree with him.

The data already bears this out. The Royal Bank of Canada does an annual survey with the business consulting arm of Capgemini Group. It found there are now 3.37 million individuals with investable assets greater than $1 million in the Asia-Pacific region. That's in contrast to 3.17 million in the EU and 3.35 million in North America.

Similarly, the *International Business Times* reported last September that ultra-wealthy global assets now reflect a combined total of $25.8 trillion, concentrated among just 187,380 individuals.

Speaking of wealth distribution around the globe...

Global Debt Statistics Illustrate a Clear Contrast

Once upon a time, the United States was the world's largest creditor. Now it's the largest debtor nation in recorded history.

After decades of incompetent fiscal management and a willingness to turn a blind eye to the long-term effects of debt and government spending, it's easy to understand what went wrong. America is backed by nothing more than made-up numbers – and debt that's sold based on those numbers.

By contrast, many Asian countries operate as creditors. Their economies are backed by real growth, real business, and ample natural resources, which are real hedges against the fantasy of European and U.S. debt.

This is clearly illustrated by statistics compiled by the International Monetary Fund (IMF), which not only ranks countries by their total debt as a function of balance-of-payments numbers, but also (since 2006) by a more interesting statistic called the "Net International Investment Position," or NIIP.

Net International Investment Position by Country	
NIIP (in millions of $)	Country
$3,087,703.98	Japan
$1,890,651.81	Republic of China
$1,386,254.30	Germany
$786,331.61	Switzerland
$693,805.13	Hong Kong
$528,836.58	Singapore
$395,909.40	Belgium
$340,021.76	Norway
$223,853.87	Netherlands
$51,340.01	Luxembourg
$27,549.11	Denmark
$19,165.16	Finland
$15,684.76	Russia
$987.17	Israel
$607.41	Malta
$230.16	Austria
-$10,025.88	Chile
-$13,916.79	Estonia
-$16,462.00	Philippines
-$17,209.33	Slovenia
-$33,975.10	Kazakhstan
-$58,476.39	Slovak Republic
-$107,615.24	Sweden
-$122,214.99	New Zealand
-$148,000.00	South Korea
-$158,600.00	India
-$200,660.09	Ireland
-$205,181.19	Canada
-$250,063.89	Portugal
-$272,932.12	France
-$275,687.00	Turkey
-$294,430.48	Greece
-$300,480.75	Poland
-$312,424.12	United Kingdom
-$362,731.69	Mexico
-$508,374.53	Italy
-$700,786.18	Brazil
-$794,884.42	Australia
-$1,233,388.16	Spain
-$2,470,989.15	United States

Source: IMF

NIIP is defined as "the difference between foreign assets owned by a country's domestic residents and institutions and the amount of domestic assets held by foreign entities."

The calculations include both public (government) debt and private debt and assets. Final figures for 2011 are still being compiled, but the rankings for 2010 – shown in the previous table – clearly define the contrast between leading Western and Asian nations. (**Note:** All figures have been adjusted to nominal U.S. dollars.)

It's no surprise that the United States is the most unbalanced country, anchoring the bottom of the list with almost $2.5 trillion less in domestically owned foreign assets than in liabilities to foreign investors.

Even more alarming is the speed with which the U.S. reached the bottom of the list. As the chart below shows, the U.S. was actually a creditor nation in terms of NIIP until 1986, but the plunge has been precipitous – and the federal government's current monetary policies and budgetary excesses demonstrate little hope that the U.S. status will improve any time soon.

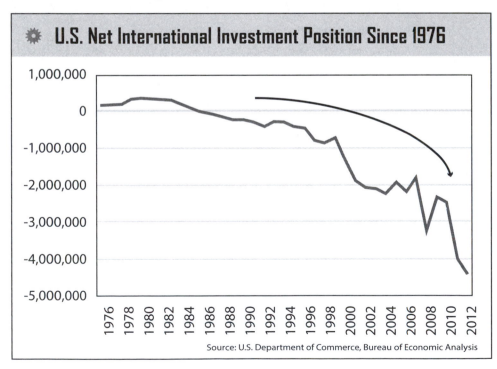

U.S. Net International Investment Position Since 1976

Source: U.S. Department of Commerce, Bureau of Economic Analysis

The same is true for the most troubled Eurozone nations – Spain, Greece, Italy, and Portugal – which also have large negative NIIP rankings.

By contrast, Japan, China, Germany, and Switzerland boast the best NIIP readings, with Hong Kong and Singapore also contributing heavily to Asia's positive creditor rankings.

While we're on the subject of debt, the Bank of International Settlements has some interesting data that factor into the Money Map Method.

Growth is seriously undermined, the BIS notes, when:

1. Government debt exceeds 100% of GDP
2. Household debt exceeds 85% of GDP
3. Corporate debt exceeds 90% of GDP

Not surprisingly, the nations currently making headlines for their fiscal follies make this list, as shown in this table:

Debt as a Percentage of GDP for Non-Financial Sectors (2010) *				
	Government	**Country**	**Household**	**Total Non-Financial**
U.S.	97	76	**95**	268
Japan	**213**	**161**	82	456
Germany	77	**100**	64	241
UK	89	**126**	**106**	321
France	97	**155**	69	321
Italy	**129**	**128**	53	310
Canada	**113**	**107**	**94**	314
Austria	82	**99**	57	238
Belgium	**115**	**185**	56	356
Finland	57	**145**	67	269
Greece	**132**	65	65	262
Netherlands	76	**121**	**130**	327
Portugal	**107**	**153**	**106**	366
Spain	72	**193**	**91**	356
Ireland	**137**	**210**	**147**	494
Critical Level	**100**	**90**	**85**	

* Countries in italics belong to the European Union. Numbers in bold are above the Critical Level.
Source: Bank of International Settlements – "Trade-Off: Financial System Supply Chain Cross -Contagion"

Key Takeaway:

The airwaves are filled with ivory tower pundits who think Japan's new loose-money policies are going to resuscitate the Japanese economy, while delivering investors a once-in-a-lifetime opportunity.

I couldn't disagree more. (And I have spent more than 20 years on the ground in that nation.) Japan's had cheap-money policies for decades, and they've done exactly squat.

The stock market will rally significantly, but unless you are nimble enough to trade it, the real opportunity is betting on a complete breakdown of the Japanese yen. Investors who followed along with my recommendation to short the yen in July 2012 (by purchasing **ProShares UltraShort Yen** (NYSEArca: YCS)) are up 61.26% (at press time). George Soros has joined in, reportedly banking more than a billion dollars doing the same thing. You can too, using any one of half a dozen methods, including YCS.

Natural Resources: Think of the Future World in Two Parts

By now, you're probably getting the idea that debt, when gone out of control, is not a good thing for your money or your country.

Well, that's entirely intentional on my part.

Our modern way of life has been built on a level of consumption that our planet cannot possibly sustain. As a result, we must begin to think of the future in two parts:

1. What the world *must* have...
2. And what it would be *nice* to have

The items in the first category are obvious: water, food, energy, medicine, and other necessities for human survival and basic comfort.

Items in the second category relate more to personal desires and present circumstances: finer clothes, faster cars, better homes, newer televisions, computers, phones, etc.

Most people see this contrast as very threatening, a reason to focus investments on dwindling resources – where prices will almost certainly rise as a function of supply/demand metrics. That's a valid viewpoint. But it overlooks an even greater opportunity.

Any time change – whether driven by the necessity of increasing population or the demand of growing human desires – accelerates so rapidly as to overwhelm the resources of the day, we see gains in creation, efficiency, and productivity.

Many people think this is optional – but it's not. We either learn to do more with less, or we wind up with not enough to go around.

And that's the greatest opportunity for both us and our money.

We must invest in those things that "move the needle to the right" – in the changes that narrow the gap between the world's remaining resources and the needs to which they are allocated.

That goes beyond the basic needs – beyond food, water, power, and basic medicines – and into the realm of advanced technology, comprehensive health-care organizations, improved transportation systems, financing mechanisms, better resource management, and, most especially, more efficient delivery systems for all of them. Even money.

Key Takeaway:

There's no question technology is going to play a big part of our future - and could make or break your portfolio. The key is investing early enough and broadly enough that you get your piece of the pie.

I've got my eye on an Israeli technology firm. It has its fingers in more than a dozen high-tech startups that will create a blizzard of new patents and products in the years ahead, while generating hundreds of millions in profits along the way. I think it's good for 400% or more in the next three to five years.

This Is Where the Money Map Method Comes In

Once you can see the truly unique forces shaping the markets, and the pressure they put on your ability to make money, then you can do something positive about it. You'll be able to recognize and take advantage of the major opportunities growing out of the massive changes taking place right now. You have the opportunity to make mega returns.

And it really is a "method" – in the truest sense of the word. There's no guesswork, no hocus-pocus, and no baloney. Just a carefully chosen, meticulously tested approach to today's markets.

So let's look at the Money Map Method itself... how it works... and what it can do for you...

The Money Map Method

Use these five strategies to restore your financial future and build real wealth.

The Money Map Method is a carefully developed, no-nonsense approach to the markets. It's for people who want to understand the world's new financial realities and capitalize on the continuing changes in order to save more, invest better, and build true wealth.

It's designed to do three things:

1. Reveal to you the ongoing transfer of social, political, and economic power away from the "nanny markets" of the West to new international commercial and business centers.

2. Demonstrate how you can save more and invest better, despite radically changing financial realities and shifting resource allocations in the decades ahead.

3. Help you build, maintain, and protect lifelong wealth and hit some huge "home runs" along the way.

It's a surprisingly simple methodology, relying on just five key strategies.

These five strategies are based on extensive research... quantitative testing of both past market performance and future economic prospects... years of personal experience by numerous professionals (including me) in every financial venue... and decades of proven success by history's most renowned investors.

So let's dig in.

1. Introducing the 50-40-10 Strategy: Higher Returns are *Absolutely* Within Your Reach

The single most important tool in The Money Map Method is **the 50-40-10 Strategy**. It's at the core of everything we do.

It's not fancy, but it's very elegant in its simplicity.

And it doesn't matter whether you have a few thousand dollars to your name or a few hundred million. You can make it work for your money.

The 50-40-10 Strategy is a way of grouping investments into three risk-adjusted tiers that correspond loosely to the layers in the "Food Pyramid" we all grew up with:

1. The bottom layer – *the 50* – is chock-full of stuff your mom probably told you to eat, but that you thought tasted like wallpaper paste.

2. The middle layer – *the 40* – includes stuff that actually tastes good and makes you want seconds because it helps you grow.

3. The top layer – *the 10* – is the beer and chips, or the chocolate mousse, depending on your taste. It's the higher-risk stuff that can easily make you fat if you eat too much. But used in the right way, it can juice your portfolio to amazing heights.

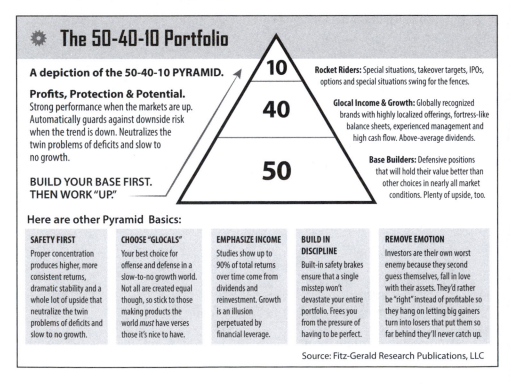

☼ The 50-40-10 Portfolio

A depiction of the 50-40-10 PYRAMID.

Profits, Protection & Potential.
Strong performance when the markets are up. Automatically guards against downside risk when the trend is down. Neutralizes the twin problems of deficits and slow to no growth.

BUILD YOUR BASE FIRST. THEN WORK "UP."

10 — **Rocket Riders:** Special situations, takeover targets, IPOs, options and special situations swing for the fences.

40 — **Glocal Income & Growth:** Globally recognized brands with highly localized offerings, fortress-like balance sheets, experienced management and high cash flow. Above-average dividends.

50 — **Base Builders:** Defensive positions that will hold their value better than other choices in nearly all market conditions. Plenty of upside, too.

Here are other Pyramid Basics:

SAFETY FIRST	CHOOSE "GLOCALS"	EMPHASIZE INCOME	BUILD IN DISCIPLINE	REMOVE EMOTION
Proper concentration produces higher, more consistent returns, dramatic stability and a whole lot of upside that neutralize the twin problems of deficits and slow to no growth.	Your best choice for offense and defense in a slow-to-no growth world. Not all are created equal though, so stick to those making products the world *must* have verses those it's nice to have.	Studies show up to 90% of total returns over time come from dividends and reinvestment. Growth is an illusion perpetuated by financial leverage.	Built-in safety brakes ensure that a single misstep won't devastate your entire portfolio. Frees you from the pressure of having to be perfect.	Investors are their own worst enemy because they second guess themselves, fall in love with their assets. They'd rather be "right" instead of profitable so they hang on letting big gainers turn into losers that put them so far behind they'll never catch up.

Source: Fitz-Gerald Research Publications, LLC

I chose the pyramid deliberately because visual representations help the brain organize abstract concepts. Rather than just spouting numbers, I've found that pictures – and particularly shapes – show investors how and where to put their money for maximum gains and minimum risk.

I also like the pyramid illustration because it's simple. One quick look and you know which side represents the bottom, which point represents the top. Visually, you understand that the higher you go "up" the pyramid, the more limited your choices become. (Try and climb one sometime and you'll see exactly what I mean.)

Even better, the pyramid forces you to "eat" healthier choices – like a blend of fish, meats, and vegetables. So it injects discipline. You don't get

---

The Money Map Philosophy

There are 11 ideas and essential truths that underlie the philosophy of the Money Map Method. Take a look:

1. The world, both financially and culturally, is rapidly changing. Once we accept the new realities, we can make money on them.

2. Deep value will trump trendy stocks every time.

3. "Timing" the markets is an exercise in futility.

4. Traditional "diversification" models are badly broken and will cost you money. The "concentration" model (50-40-10) is the only effective way to build lasting wealth.

5. Income plays a far bigger role than appreciation when it comes to growing your wealth.

6. Fast gains are great, but investors need a "lifetime income plan."

7. All investing involves risk – but not all risks are the same. You can reduce risk and still get high returns.

8. Bear tracks always come before the running of the bulls.

9. Structure ("where" you invest your money) is much more important than the individual stocks you buy.

10. Sitting on the sidelines in tumultuous times may feel good, but it is absolutely the wrong thing to do.

11. The 24-hour financial news cycle is replete with misinformation. Ignore the hype and stick with a proven strategy.

---

the chance to pile on everything from chips to sodas in a gluttonous orgy – one that feels good at the time, but you always end up regretting.

I mention this because many investors wind up with far too many speculative choices on their investment plate. They get caught up in emotional investing that can wreak havoc with their serious money – money meant for the long term. Not surprisingly, that's when investors who think they're "investing" find out the hard way that they're blindly speculating.

Unfortunately, they find this out by getting slammed around when the markets turn foul. That's primarily because their risk is disproportionately concentrated, even though their broker may convince them that their "diversified" portfolio is somehow "safer."

What's in the 50-40-10?

The three tiers of the pyramid shown in the graphic on the previous page represent the three distinct elements of the Money Map Strategy:

Base Builders – We allocate 50% of our investment capital to assets chosen because of both their stability and their income-producing potential. This provides a safe foundation that will better withstand downturns, while also giving us a solid base from which to pursue growth.

Growth and Income Holdings – 40% of our funds are invested in this category, typically targeting "glocal" (global + local) companies that provide the potential for capital appreciation, as well as income in the form of above-average dividend yields.

Rocket Riders – At this higher-risk level, we invest up to 10% of our capital in assets that offer greater growth potential based on some sort of catalyst our research has uncovered. Examples may include new patents, contracts, buyouts, spinoffs, etc.

If you think focusing on safety, steady growth, and income, while using only 10% of our capital to "swing for the fences" sounds like we're leaving too much opportunity on the table, then think again.

By distributing our holdings using the 50-40-10 Strategy, we are also *distributing our risk* more effectively than traditional diversification models do.

Does the approach work? You bet it does – and to show you how well it works, I constructed a hypothetical $10,000 portfolio using just 11 choices that I split up according to the 50-40-10 Strategy, as follows:

Components	Ticker	Initial Weighting at Top of Each Year
Base Builders		
Vanguard Wellington Fund	VWELX	15%
Nuveen Quality Income Municipal Fund	NQU	10%
Vanguard Inflation-Protected Securities Fund	VIPSX	10%
PIMCO Strategic Global Government Fund	RCS	10%
Gold	Gold	5%
Growth and Income		
Kinder Morgan Energy Partners, L.P.	KMP	10%
Altria Group Inc.	MO	10%
Vanguard International Explorer Fund	VINEX	10%
Vanguard Selected Value Fund	VASVX	10%
Rocket Riders		
Vanguard Small-Cap Value Fund	VISVX	5%
Vanguard Emerging Markets Stock Index Fund	VEIEX	5%

I let it run from August 1, 2000, to April 11, 2012, and I rebalanced annually on the first trading day of each year, using adjusted closing prices from Yahoo! Finance and Kitco Precious Metals to keep things simple.

I chose those dates for two reasons: 1) I hear constantly from people who are worried that the sky is falling; 2) I also hear from those who tell me with a straight face that there's nothing to invest in right now – and that there hasn't been for years.

During this time, our markets experienced several wars, recessions, the dot.bomb crash, two meltdowns, three melt-ups, numerous political crack-ups, the current financial mess, and more.

As you can see from the next graphic, this simple 50-40-10 Strategy absolutely crushed the S&P 500.

To be precise, between August 1, 2000, and April 11, 2012, while the S&P 500 lost -4.83%, our 50-40-10 Strategy would have returned a whopping 238.88%!

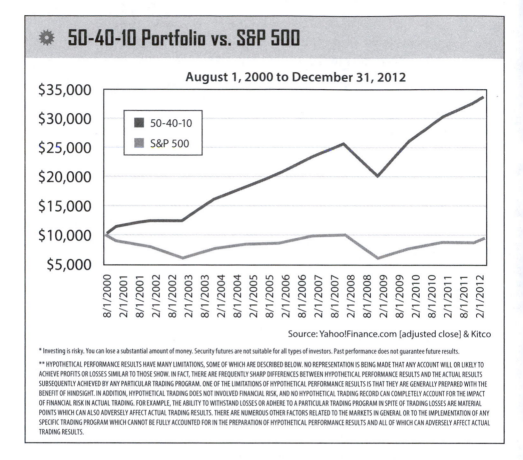

☀ 50-40-10 Portfolio vs. S&P 500

August 1, 2000 to December 31, 2012

Legend:
- 50-40-10
- S&P 500

Source: Yahoo!Finance.com [adjusted close] & Kitco

* Investing is risky. You can lose a substantial amount of money. Security futures are not suitable for all types of investors. Past performance does not guarantee future results.

** HYPOTHETICAL PERFORMANCE RESULTS HAVE MANY LIMITATIONS, SOME OF WHICH ARE DESCRIBED BELOW. NO REPRESENTATION IS BEING MADE THAT ANY ACCOUNT WILL OR LIKELY TO ACHIEVE PROFITS OR LOSSES SIMILAR TO THOSE SHOW. IN FACT, THERE ARE FREQUENTLY SHARP DIFFERENCES BETWEEN HYPOTHETICAL PERFORMANCE RESULTS AND THE ACTUAL RESULTS SUBSEQUENTLY ACHIEVED BY ANY PARTICULAR TRADING PROGRAM. ONE OF THE LIMITATIONS OF HYPOTHETICAL PERFORMANCE RESULTS IS THAT THEY ARE GENERALLY PREPARED WITH THE BENEFIT OF HINDSIGHT. IN ADDITION, HYPOTHETICAL TRADING DOES NOT INVOLVED FINANCIAL RISK, AND NO HYPOTHETICAL TRADING RECORD CAN COMPLETELY ACCOUNT FOR THE IMPACT OF FINANCIAL RISK IN ACTUAL TRADING. FOR EXAMPLE, THE ABILITY TO WITHSTAND LOSSES OR ADHERE TO A PARTICULAR TRADING PROGRAM IN SPITE OF TRADING LOSSES ARE MATERIAL POINTS WHICH CAN ALSO ADVERSELY AFFECT ACTUAL TRADING RESULTS. THERE ARE NUMEROUS OTHER FACTORS RELATED TO THE MARKETS IN GENERAL OR TO THE IMPLEMENTATION OF ANY SPECIFIC TRADING PROGRAM WHICH CANNOT BE FULLY ACCOUNTED FOR IN THE PREPARATION OF HYPOTHETICAL PERFORMANCE RESULTS AND ALL OF WHICH CAN ADVERSELY AFFECT ACTUAL TRADING RESULTS.

*I quickly updated the model to reflect where we stand as of our second printing and the numbers are even more impressive: 287.54%.

Nothing against people who tell me they are worried, or those who fear event-driven market madness... But history shows there is a way around almost every market obstacle. It just may require a big leap of faith on your part.

Until you let go of the concept that spreading your money around willy nilly, using classic diversification modeling, you are at the mercy of unseen risks, not to mention emotional hang-ups, that will override what you logically understand about the world we presently live in and the opportunities being created right now... opportunities that exist despite everything troublesome that's going on.

I get this question a lot: Can you improve the 50-40-10's performance still further?

You bet you can.

For example, you could rebalance more often – semi-annually or even quarterly – when interest rates are rising. This will help capture more rapid rises in equities that are usually associated with rising rates. You could rebalance even less frequently when rates are falling to capture the appreciation associated with bond markets.

Or you could effectively harvest gains by using trailing stops or put options to safeguard your capital from catastrophic losses while also grabbing partial profits when the markets are "peakish."

Here's one of my favorite tactics: Simply add new money when market conditions are conducive to deep-value investments and showing plenty of upside.

Incidentally, I recommend all these as they apply to specific recommendations in my newsletter, *The Money Map Report*.

Yet here you're going to go deeper than I've ever revealed before about exactly how this all works. Here are more of the simple tactics I use for my readers – and you can use too – to boost returns even higher.

Let's begin with income.

2. Dividends and Income Make Superior Returns Possible

Many people are surprised to learn that dividend income and reinvestment can account for nearly 90% of total stock market returns over time.

That's right. Not a quarter... Not half... But 90%.

That's why placing a high priority on dividends in the 50-40-10 Strategy is paramount to its success.

Unfortunately, this goes counter to the inclinations of far too many investors. They spend the bulk of their time chasing "the next hot stock" or searching for the next "sure thing."

No doubt we all love the elation that goes with being up 25%, 50%, 100%, or more.

Don't get me wrong, though. I'll take gains like that too – and we get more than our fair share, as you'll see in *The Money Map Report* model portfolio. Yet when it comes to consistently growing and protecting our money, I'd rather focus on getting the cold, hard cash that dividends kick off. That's because I know those are a much bigger component of overall investment returns over time.

I point this out because what most people fail realize is that successful investing is a matter of continuous performance – NOT instantaneous performance.

Here's where it gets really interesting.

In some cases, the dividends are so steady and increase so much that over time you can actually make more in dividends than you originally paid to buy the stocks that produced them.

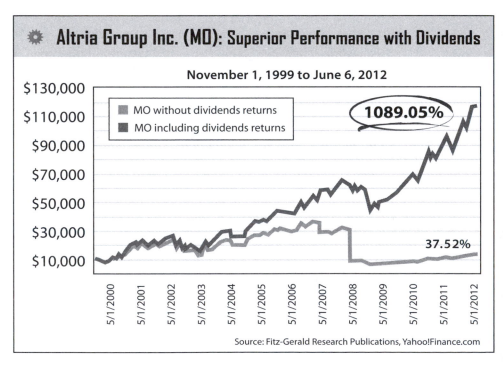

❖ **Altria Group Inc. (MO): Superior Performance with Dividends**

November 1, 1999 to June 6, 2012

- MO without dividends returns
- MO including dividends returns

1089.05%

37.52%

Source: Fitz-Gerald Research Publications, Yahoo!Finance.com

Two of the founding fathers of modern investing made that abundantly clear in the 1930s.

Benjamin Graham and David Dodd pointed out in their seminal work, *Security Analysis* (1934), that dividends were the primary contributing factors to long-term total return.

A few years later, John Burr Williams noted in his book, *The Theory of Investment Value* (1938), that "a stock is worth the present value of all the dividends ever to be paid upon it, no more, no less."

If you don't believe those assertions, ask anyone who invested in **Altria Group Inc.** (NYSE:MO) over the past 12 years if they'd disagree. They've enjoyed total returns north of 1,000%.

Folks who've held **Kinder Morgan Energy Partners LP** (NYSE:KMP) or **Reynolds American Inc.** (NYSE:RAI) over the same time frame have seen total returns of 1,578% and 3,311%, respectively – with returns from dividends far exceeding capital gains in both cases.

Not bad for having held through an extraordinarily difficult decade that a lot of investors wrote off as "uninvestable."

There will be plenty of trying times ahead just like the past 12 years – and once again, it will be dividends that maximize your returns.

> ### Dividends Pay in the Short Term, Too
>
> In the 12 months ending August 31, 2012, S&P 500 companies that pay dividends outperformed non-dividend payers by more than 9 percentage points.
>
> According to Standard & Poor's, stocks that pay dividends rose by more than 5%, while non-payers were down by about 4%.

Granted, building wealth through dividends takes time – but time is the one guaranteed asset you have to work with. Instead of constantly trying to cheat it, learn to work with it.

Chances are excellent that your money will thank you.

In fact, working *with* time is a key element of the third strategy employed in the Money Map Method – investing in real value.

Key Takeaway:

Many investors have thrown up their hands since the financial crisis began saying that there's nothing to invest in. Nothing could be farther from the trust, especially if you learn how to harvest gains using our "free-trade" method.

Here's how it works.

I recommend my subscribers sell one-half of their position in a stock or fund whenever it doubles (and keep the remaining half open). This is called a "free trade," because you not only get back your original investment, *but you maintain all the upside you can handle, essentially "for free."*

My philosophy is, ...hey, why not take your original investment off the table... let the gains continue to pile up, while you play with "the house's money"... and reinvest that money into new potentially profitable picks?

This is a tactic drawn directly from more than three decades in the market. It's one that individual investors typically don't know about but can – and should – use to their great advantage.

Case in point, I recommended **Altria Group Inc.** (NYSE: MO) to subscribers in February 2010. Those who followed along sold half their position in July 2012 and captured total returns of more than 100%. So they not only paid for their initial investment, but created a "free trade" in the process.

3. Never Pay Full Price for Anything

Let me ask you a rhetorical question: Would you go to a 50% *more* sale at your favorite department store?

Probably not.

Yet that's exactly what many investors do every day. They buy into stocks, bonds, commodities, and all sorts of things when the markets are "expensive" – and they sell when they're not.

They should be doing just the opposite.

Buying "on the cheap" is an important part of the Money Map Method. Doing so gives us that much more upside. In fact, it can give us triple-digit potential when seemingly nothing else works.

Some people hear this and think I'm advocating market timing. I'm not!

What I'm pointing out is that **the markets have a distinct upward bias over time**. This means that identifying periods of relative undervalue and capitalizing on them can lead to bigger returns. That's because the conditions favor buying over selling, especially if you use what I'm about to tell you as part of a risk-parity strategy like the 50-40-10.

Remember the following chart from earlier in the book? You can clearly see the pronounced upward trend over time I just mentioned. You can also see that there were times over history (1920, 1932, 1949, 1982, and 2009) when it paid to "back up the truck" and buy.

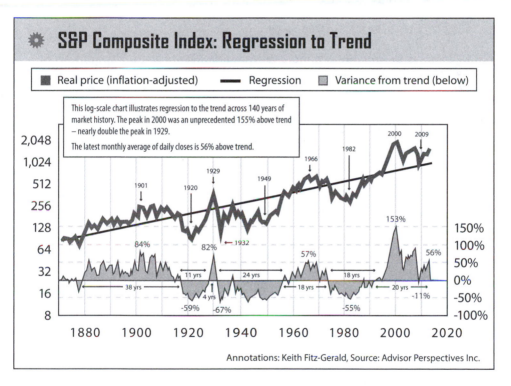

I point this out for one reason. Understanding where we are in the scheme of things can help you overcome several of our biggest challenges right now: ineffective regulation, feckless leaders pursuing populist agendas, baling-wire bailouts, unprecedented debt, and the inevitability of higher taxes.

Most investors think in terms of bulls and bears, so they are stunned – shocked is more like it – when I tell them that the markets go absolutely nowhere for long periods of time.

In fact, over the last 115 years, there have really only been four major bull markets, lasting an average of 10.5 years and producing an average gain of 397.18%. There have also been four bear/sideways markets, lasting an average of 17.5 years and producing an average gain of 2.33%.

The proverbial bottom line is this: Buying when the markets demonstrate deep value is one of the easiest and most consistently profitable approaches available to investors today.

Deep value is most usually found when the markets are either 1) beaten down or 2) going nowhere.

The Five Steps to Finding Deep Value

Finding deep value is not complicated. In fact, value really consists of just five basic elements:

1. Efficiency
2. Mean reversion
3. Margin of safety
4. Screening
5. Patience and discipline

Step No. 1: Understand Efficiency

Contrary to what people believe, efficiency has nothing to do with price.

Efficiency speaks to what happens millions of times a day around the world when stocks get bought and sold. It presumes that one party in the transactions is always wrong. The trick, of course, is not being that person.

In order to be successful, you've got to presume that other people are irrational and that they don't see what you see. That speaks to the need for careful selection (which we'll talk about in a few pages).

Another important thing to understand, when it comes to efficiency, is that it's less important to pick specific stocks than it is to be on the right side of the trade. That's why, when you apply this methodology, you must be consistent.

Finally, never forget that, when it comes to making efficient investments, finding bargains is your ultimate objective – especially if you are using the 50-40-10 risk-parity strategy.

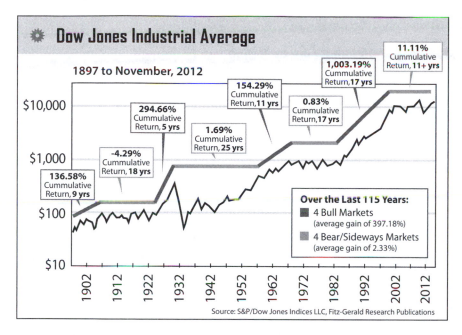

Not to belabor the issue, but the whole point is to identify stocks that others don't yet see for what they are – diamonds in the rough.

Admittedly, this sounds a lot like contrarian investing, but that's actually not the case. Finding cheap stocks is not the same thing. Contrarians are great at picking tops and bottoms; the rest of the time, as the adage goes, they are just wrong.

This kind of investing, when done the Money Map Method way, presumes that we are hunting for something we actually want to own – not something that has merely been thrown out with the bath water.

That said, I love finding companies that are anomalies: boring, ugly, or bruised-and-battered... sometimes all of the above. They're hard to find, but when seen clearly, they're worth big money.

Another thing I love about value as a part of the Money Map Method is that you don't have to be absolutely right to make sizable gains.

Not only are there more opportunities, but the sweet spot for those opportunities is dramatically bigger and deeper than in forms of investing that focus on other elements – momentum, growth, or growth at a reasonable price, for example.

That's because things always return to their mean.

Step No. 2: Know How Mean Reversion Works

Mean reversion is the mathematical expression of a widely documented natural phenomenon: *Prices will return to their mean over time.*

Think of how water behaves. After being disturbed, in time, it self-levels. Or consider a rubber band. After being stretched to its limit, it will recoil to its original shape.

You can see mean reversion at work in stock market data, too, for major averages like the Dow and the S&P 500 – or in practically any tradable index, for that matter. There are short periods when this relationship is disturbed, but generally speaking, my studies show the concept of mean reversion is a truism over time – just like the sun coming up tomorrow or the grass turning green in spring.

What's more, mean reversion is extremely consistent in all market conditions. That's why, with very few exceptions:

- Bull markets start when prices are **below** mean valuations and end at levels higher than mean valuations.

- Bear markets and sideways markets start when prices are **above** mean valuations and end at lower-than-mean valuations.

The latter, my second bullet point, is where we are now – and the reason why so many investors are struggling. They simply cannot get it through their heads that the big rallies they desperately want to see on the horizon to make up lost ground are highly unlikely. Not impossible, mind you. Just unlikely.

That means we have to plan our investments accordingly, with an even greater emphasis on value and the risk-parity protection offered by the 50-40-10 Strategy. That's especially true when it comes to putting new money to work.

Key Takeaway:

Most investors are at least passingly familiar with "mean reversion." Putting the concept to work can definitely help you find great companies that are trading at steep discounts. It can also be used to start assembling insurance, in the form of inverse mutual funds or ETFs, when the market is looking toppish.

Which brings us to something called the "margin of safety."

Steps No. 3 and 4: Get Higher Potential Returns and a Buffer against Loss

According to Benjamin Graham, who is regarded as the Godfather of Value Investing, the "margin of safety" is the price at which a share investment can be purchased at minimal risk. Usually, that means shares are "underpriced."

I prefer to think of it in even simpler terms...

The bigger your margin of safety, the higher your potential gain and the safer your money is against loss.

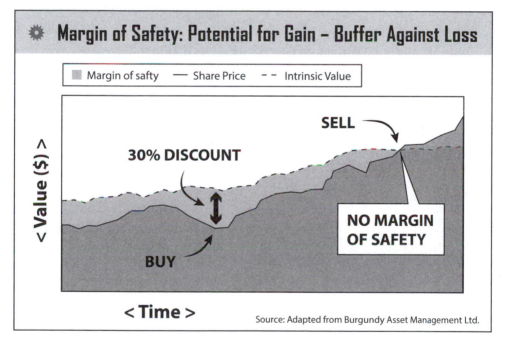

Margin of Safety: Potential for Gain – Buffer Against Loss

Margin of safty · — Share Price · − − Intrinsic Value

< Value ($) >

SELL

30% DISCOUNT

NO MARGIN OF SAFETY

BUY

< Time >

Source: Adapted from Burgundy Asset Management Ltd.

The converse is true too. If a stock is significantly above its margin of safety, you can wait until it pulls back a bit. Or, if you're an aggressive trader, consider shorting it.

Of course, what goes up must come down: The concept of mean reversion works in reverse, too.

But how do you find the opportunities?

Frankly, it doesn't matter whether you use crystal balls, Pepsi bottles, or voodoo bones, so long as you have a method you understand and which you can consistently apply to all market conditions. What's important is that you have a means of identifying things that others cannot yet see.

That's where the Money Map Method comes in (as you'll see in a moment). It gives you an edge over millions of investors seeking the same thing.

For example, I recommended **Rydex Inverse S&P Strategy Fund (RYURX)** – a specialized inverse fund that moves up when the S&P 500 moves down – to *Money Map Report* subscribers in December 2007, shortly after the S&P 500 hit its previous all-time high. Subscribers who followed along exited the position 17 months later for a 28.92% gain. Those who didn't had to endure an unpleasant white-knuckle ride and had nothing to show for it, least of all profits.

We'll talk about some of the key methods of determining value, establishing a margin of safety, and gaining that edge in just a second, but first a quick word about the final elements required for success as a value investor: patience and discipline.

Step No. 5: Patience and Discipline

While it is possible to make a lot of money in the short term, the longer-term trends that are just getting started will be worth far more over time – and carry much less risk.

You just need the patience to go along for the full ride... and the discipline not to lose faith and too quickly grab the money and run.

Discipline also comes into play in terms of repeat performance. While it's alright to "fine tune" your methods, you don't want to mess with success too much. Once you have a valuation method that you understand – and that has proven itself under varying market conditions – stick with it. Don't go looking for something "better" any time you hear tales (most likely exaggerated) of someone who scored bigger, faster profits or made more substantial returns. Trust your method.

Screening: Three Formulas that Get the Job Done

Thank goodness for technology. It's certainly made my life myriad times easier.

The screening process used to involve days of hard work and plenty of pencil lead. Today, any investor can screen literally thousands of stocks in minutes.

There's just one caveat: Whereas most investors view this as an advantage, I really don't.

In fact, I think that, unless you really know what you are looking for, most computers simply allow us to make more informed mistakes.

That's why I encourage people interested in investing to take a few minutes and look "under the hood" of the methods and formulas you use. This is kind of like proving to your professor you understand the math before he or she allows you to use a calculator. I actually had to do that in finance class – but that's a story for another time.

The important thing is that you know what's behind the formula you're using – and why.

I actually have three favorite "buy-it-cheap" formulas that can help me find screaming value. I don't just apply them in isolation, however.

Before I even get to the point where I am looking to place new money or rebalance what I have, I use the 50-40-10 Strategy to determine exactly what holes I have to fill and with how much money. That way, if the screens driven by these formulas kick out a bunch of choices that don't "fit," I'm under no obligation to act. In fact, when that happens, I interpret that as a sign that I shouldn't do anything.

Let's start with the granddaddy of all stock screens...

Graham's Intrinsic Value

Benjamin Graham believed he could apply a series of market data and company-specific variables criteria to evaluate a stock's intrinsic value.

His original formula was quite simple, but it required any analyst using it to make some serious SWAGs (**S**cientific **W**ild **A**** **G**uesses). Here's the formula:

$$V* = EPS \times (8.5 + 2g)$$

V = Intrinsic Value
EPS = Trailing 12-months earnings per share
8.5 = PE base for a no-growth company
g = Reasonably expected 7- to 10-year growth rate

According to analysts I talked with early in my career, the problem with this formula was that a company with an expected 10% growth rate, for example, could have a PE of 28.5 and still be considered a buy. Fully 50% of the S&P 500 met these criteria at the time, although the PE was, in fact, much lower.

To Graham's way of thinking, any company that could maintain this growth rate for decades would actually be a bargain.

Graham revised this formula in 1974 in his second book, "The Decade 1965-1974: Its Significance for Financial Analysts," as noted here:

$$V* = \frac{EPS \times (8.5 + 2g) \times 4.4}{Y}$$

V = Intrinsic Value
EPS = Trailing 12-months earnings per share
8.5 = Appropriate PE base for a no-growth company as proposed by Graham
g = Reasonably expected five-year growth-rate estimate
4.4 = The average yield of high-grade corporate bonds in 1962, when this model was introduced
Y = The current yield on AAA corporate bonds

To apply this model to a buy-sell decision, each company's relative Graham value (RGV) can be determined by dividing the stock's intrinsic value (V*) by its current price (P):

$$RGV = \frac{V*}{P}$$

An RGV greater than one (RGV > 1) indicates an **undervalued** stock that **should be bought**.

An RGV less than one (RGV < 1) indicates an **overvalued** stock that **should not be bought – or should be shorted**.

You'll notice a couple of interesting things.

First, there was no interest-rate assumption in the original model, yet there was in the second. He added that.

Next, Graham distilled this to a single decision-making variable – RGV – so the formula became a lot more usable. To reiterate, any RGV greater than one indicates an undervalued stock; less than one suggests a stock is overvalued.

The downside to this model is that it assumes a constant EPS growth – which, as millions of investors have figured out the hard way, doesn't mean much in the highly manipulated markets we deal with today as compared with the calmer, more civilized markets of Graham's day.

Another caveat, if you're going to use Graham's screen: You must take several important external factors into consideration in conjunction with the data you produce. These include current assets, which help determine short-term viability; the debt-to-equity ratio; and the quality of management.

So there's room for some subjectivity.

Here's another model I like very much.

The Piotroski Score

This one was created and introduced by former University of Chicago Professor Joseph Piotroski and first presented in a paper published in 2000 titled, "Value Investing: The Use of Historical Financial Information to Separate Winners from Losers."

Like Graham, Piotroski believes the concept of valuation can be used as a determinative factor in picking investments. He uses a nine-point methodology that simplistically awards a "point" for each acceptable or "passing" criterion, as follows:[1]

1. **Net Income:** Bottom line. Score 1 if the last year's net income is positive.

2. **Operating Cash Flow:** A better earnings gauge. Score 1 if the last year's cash flow is positive.

3. **Return on Assets:** Measures profitability. Score 1 if the last year's ROA exceeds the prior-year ROA.

4. **Quality of Earnings:** Warns of accounting tricks. Score 1 if the last year's operating cash flow exceeds net income.

5. **Long-Term Debt versus Assets:** Is debt decreasing? Score 1 if the ratio of long-term debt to assets is down from the year-ago value. (If LTD is zero, but assets are increasing, score 1 anyway.)

6. **Current Ratio:** Measures increasing working capital. Score 1 if CR has increased from the prior year.

7. **Shares Outstanding:** A measure of potential dilution. Score 1 if the number of shares outstanding is no greater than the year-ago figure.

8. **Gross Margin:** A measure of improving competitive position. Score 1 if full-year GM exceeds the prior-year's GM.

9. **Asset Turnover:** Measures productivity. Score 1 if the percentage increase in sales exceeds the percentage increase in total assets.

This formula attempted to eliminate the weaknesses in other value screening methods – including, presumably, Graham's intrinsic-value approach.

Piotroski's research found that stocks rated an 8 or 9 were strongest, and significantly outperformed the broader markets – on average, by 10% a year from 1876 to 1996. Modern back-testing shows the figure varies a bit, from 7% to 11%, depending on the methodology used. But the point is that there is still a significant edge here. That's why I like the Piotroski Score a lot as it applies to the 50-40-10 Strategy.

At the other end of the spectrum, companies whose stocks had Piotroski ratings of 2 points or less were five times more likely to delist or go bankrupt.

Finally, there's a model called **Negative Enterprise Value**. Not too many people are even aware this one exists, which makes it that much more valuable to my way of thinking.

Key Takeaway:

There are two things to remember from the Piotroski score.

1. First, the strategy can find undervalued companies not yet on Wall Street's radar, though in today's highly computerized world, this is becoming less apparent – or at least the window is closing quickly.

2. Second, it recognizes the fact that many undervalued companies are trading that way because they are trash, unworthy of investment – a refinement that Graham's methods don't allow for.

Negative Enterprise Value

This model is based on the assumption that there are beaten-up companies out there with cash on hand that far outweighs their level of debt. These are typically companies that the markets have dismissed or frown upon for some reason, but that have a high level of what's known as "enterprise value," determined as follows:

Enterprise value = market cap + total debt – excess cash

This formula is an effective way to identify non-capital-intensive companies with no debt or manageable debt. It typically gives you a pretty good list of buy candidates – cash-rich companies that are trading for less than their value. In fact, I like filtering both the Graham and Piotroski results against enterprise value to sort out the trash from the potential trinkets.

Using Yahoo's screener, here's the set-up I like a lot:

Enterprise value < $50 million
Enterprise value/revenue ≤ 1
Return on Equity (ROE) ≥ 0

A Quick Look at the Results

So why would I select these three screening methods when there are literally hundreds of tools available? It's simple: they're well documented and, perhaps more importantly, consistent, too.

That means each of the methods is repeatable. It also means they can be back-tested in isolation over just about any time period you can imagine.

For example, take a look at the accompanying three charts. They show back-tested results for each of the methods I've just described.

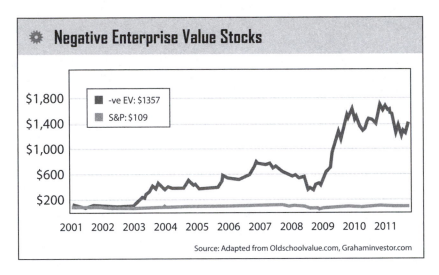

Source: Adapted from Oldschoolvalue.com, Grahaminvestor.com

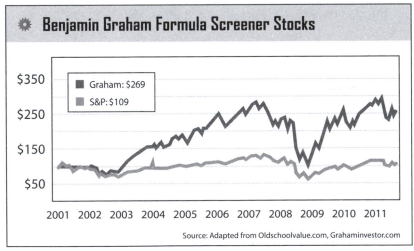

Source: Adapted from Oldschoolvalue.com, Grahaminvestor.com

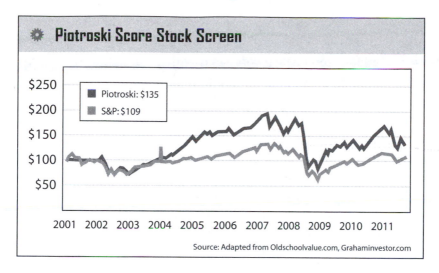

Source: Adapted from Oldschoolvalue.com, Grahaminvestor.com

Now a caveat. Many investors are going to look at those tempting upper lines and think to themselves, "Wow! These methods thrashed the market!"

That's good – and they did – but before you rush to call your broker, take a REAL look at them. Every single one of the lines reflecting the results of these methods looks like a snake. There are ups and downs and squiggles that may give you heart palpitations along the way.

Key Takeaway:

I love stock screens because they help me find companies that others may miss, either because they are simply buying hot tips or focusing on the headlines. Right now, that's the situation with regard to energy.

People have thrown energy companies out with the bathwater when, in fact, the data reflects strong growth and very appealing fundamentals. I've identified two with superb potential. Both companies have operations all around the world and their products are in high demand now that global oil and gas capital expenditures reached nearly $1 trillion in 2012. I also like the fact that their value score is head and shoulders above their peer group. That gives them a healthy margin of safety compared to alternatives.

I'm tracking similar choices in other industries, too, including medical tech, 21st-century technology, global infrastructure, water resources, global food demand, and more...

That's precisely why I combine them with what we know about the advantages of risk-parity modeling, the 50-40-10 Strategy, income, and the disciplined use of tools like trailing stops.

Because I don't like surprises... And because I also know that the more exposure the 50-40-10 Strategy has to value-oriented buys, the higher the returns are likely to be when compared with both classically diversified portfolios and the broader markets in general.

Here's one more technique you can use to ensure you never again pay full price when buying a stock: selling put options.

Sell Put Options While You Wait

Sometimes your screens will identify a potential bargain purchase, but the timing won't be right, either because the price is still a hair too high or because overall market conditions argue against new entries at the moment.

When that happens, most people do one of two things:

1. Wait patiently for conditions or the price to improve, providing an optimum entry opportunity; or,

2. Go ahead and buy at the present price and use stop-loss orders to control and limit the risk.

However, there's a third approach that I actually prefer:

3. Whenever possible, sell an out-of-the-money put option on the stock you're looking to purchase.

For those unfamiliar with options, a put gives its owner the right to sell a given security at a specific price for a limited period of time. In other words, when you sell one, you give the buyer the right to "put" 100 shares of the stock to you at the specified price, called the strike or striking price, at any time up until the option's expiration date.

For example, let's say your screens indicated **JPMorgan Chase & Co.** (NYSE:JPM) would be undervalued at a price below $43 a share, but the stock was still sitting at $44 and the broad market was moving lower.

You could do three things. You could simply wait for the market to turn or JPM to break below $43, perhaps entering a lowball order. You could go ahead and buy at $44 and limit your loss with a stop order. My preferred choice would be to sell a near-term JPM $43 put option. Here's why:

- With five weeks of life left, that near-term put would carry a premium of about $1.50 a share, or $150 for a full 100-share option contract – money you could immediately put in your pocket.

- If JPMorgan drops below the $43 strike price, you have to buy the stock at $43 a share – but your effective cost is actually $41.50 ($43.00 minus the $1.50 put premium you received). Thus, on a cost basis, you've purchased JPM below the "undervalued" price you wanted in the first place.

- If JPMorgan stays above the $43 strike price of the put, it expires worthless – and you keep the $150, then repeat the process with the next near-term put, pocketing another $150 or so. Repeat twice, and you can reduce your effective cost on JPM to $38.50 ($43.00 - $1.50 - $1.50 - $1.50 = $38.50), an extremely undervalued level.

- If JPMorgan rallies, you miss buying at the "bargain" price below $43 – which it never reached anyhow – but you still make a five-week return of 3.48% on the $4,300 you'd have paid to buy the stock (which you'd have to leave on deposit to secure the put sale). Annualized, that's an extremely appealing 35.4%.

Essentially, it's as close to a no-lose situation as you can get in the markets.

(**Note:** We say to sell puts "whenever possible" because options are not traded on every stock – especially some foreign shares, ADRs, or lower-priced issues, for example.)

These next two strategies go hand in hand.

4. Harvest Your Profits, and
5. Strictly Limit Your Losses

Too many investors become so focused on their losers that they have no idea how their winners are performing ... until they become losers. Then they start paying attention to them.

As far as I am concerned, that's just plain backwards. What they should be doing is watching their winners and figuring out how to harvest their profits.

Doing that is an important part of the Money Map Method. Consistently selling our winners allows us to continually recycle our capital into new opportunities and also accelerate our rebalancing.

If you were raised under the old axiom of "cut your losses and let your winners run," this may seem counterintuitive. But it's really no different than what happens in the produce department at the grocery store. The produce manager always replenishes the tomatoes and other fruits and vegetables to keep them fresh.

You should do the same with the "inventory" in your portfolio. If you let your stocks sit on the shelf too long, they'll eventually go bad – just like fruit that's past its expiration date.

But how do you know what to sell? And when?

Here are a few of my favorite tactics to help you lock in profits instead of letting irrational behavior and emotion take over when the markets suddenly have a mind of their own.

a) Recognize That Every Day Is a New Day

This one is very simple. If the original reasons you bought something are no longer true, ditch it – win, lose, or draw.

You can't risk falling in love with your assets, any more than you can let them rust – yet that's exactly what most investors do. They buy something, then assume that it will somehow plod along on autopilot.

This is a variation of what I call the "greater fool theory" – as in, some greater fool is going to come along at a yet-to-be-determined point in the future and pay you more for a given investment than you paid to buy it. I can't imagine what these folks are thinking.

Today, more than ever before, you've got to continually re-evaluate your investments to ensure that they stand on their own merits and are worth the risk of continued ownership.

b) Sell into Strength

Most investors have been taught to let their winners run. But ask yourself this: Why do the professionals take money off the table whenever they've got winners on their hands?

52

Bull runs out of gas!

Answer: They know that the longer a bull runs, the higher the odds of a reversal.

That's why they begin "lightening up" – systematically selling portions of their holdings, or even entire positions – when prices are rising.

We follow the same philosophy at Money Map Press.

Investors who have grown used to the "set-it-and-forget-it" approach typically don't like this method. They argue that they'll leave too much money on the table if something keeps going up. And, of course, they're absolutely correct. Selling prematurely *can* lead to reduced profits.

But what I am talking about has nothing to do with selling early.

Systematic selling when the markets are rising and liquidity is high helps you:

a) Lock in profits before a reversal arrives, and

b) Reduce the potential for future losses when that inevitable reversal does occur.

But what if the markets continue to rally?

I hear that all the time, and it's a logical question – but my answer is always the same... So what?

If a rally has legs, there's nothing to stop you from redeploying your gains into new and even better opportunities – into positions that haven't yet had the big run-up that gave you the profits you took. When those issues rally, you'll know how to manage those gains, too.

c) Use Trailing Stops

This moves into the realm of strategy No. 5, and it sounds pretty self-explanatory. However, you'd be amazed at how many people I talk with every year who don't use stops – despite the fact that most brokerages and online trading platforms have these features built in and available for free.

Trailing stops are essentially price targets that work in reverse.

They are typically calculated as a percentage of purchase price. For instance, a 25% trailing stop on **Apple Inc.** (NasdaqGS:AAPL) at $520 is $390. If the stock dropped to $390, the order would execute and carry you out of the trade automatically.

Variations include specific dollar-based stop losses (sell when it hits $390), calendar stops (sell after 12 months), and contingency orders (if it falls to $390, that triggers an order to sell put $350 options). And more.

What turns a stop, regardless of the variation, into a "trailing stop" is that the exit price increases in lock step as the current market price of your investment rises. Using the same example of Apple... If you bought at $520 and the computer maker's stock climbed to, say, $588, you'd raise your stop from $390.18 to $441, which would represent a 25% pullback from $588.

If Apple then went on to say, $700, you'd again move the stop up, this time to $525 – thereby locking in a profit of at least $5 if prices took a big tumble. (Actually, you would typically adjust your stop more frequently and in smaller increments – say $10 to $15 at a time, on a high-flyer like Apple, or $3 to $5 at a time on stocks priced below $100.)

What I like about trailing stops is that they offer an unemotional, unbiased exit path when any stock or other investment begins to move against you. Of course, that's also the catch. You have to give up some ground before you're stopped out of a trade.

As is the case with any investment strategy, there are people who don't like trailing stops because they get bounced out of trades that then seem to immediately turn around and head higher without them.

I can't say I blame them. Floor traders, hyperactive day traders, and "quants" (with computers that would make NASA envious) love to "shake the monkeys from the trees" and "run the stops." Both are euphemisms for deliberate actions intended to exploit the protective actions of others for gain.

However, that's a risk you take with any investment in today's markets. It generally doesn't bother me because I have an investor's mentality. The

Question — These move automatically?
(either way)?

daily volatility associated with this kind of gamesmanship is just "noise." Hitting the occasional stop is simply part of the game.

It's also far less painful than the major losses you can take if the daily "noise" turns out to be the start of a major correction and you aren't protected by stops.

(**Note:** If I'm day trading, that's another matter entirely – and a subject for another time because setting trailing stops in a day-trading environment is a discipline all its own.)

d) Buy Put Options

Earlier, we talked about selling put options as a means of getting into a position at a bargain price. Puts can also be an extremely useful tool in protecting against losses or locking in profits.

Buying put options is a more sophisticated variation of a trailing stop. It gives you better control over the exit process – i.e., ownership of a put means you'll be able to sell your position at the option's striking price, regardless of how far below that level the stock's market price might fall. The drawback is that the cost of your investment goes up, because you're effectively buying "insurance" against a loss.

For example, if you bought 100 shares of **Facebook Inc.** (NasdaqGS:FB) at $27 and wanted to limit your losses to 25% of your purchase price, you could place a trailing stop at $20.25 a share. Your initial investment would be $2,700 (ignoring commissions and fees for the sake of simplicity), and you'd be selling your shares automatically if the stock dropped to that point.

Or, you could buy 100 shares of Facebook today at $27 and simultaneously purchase a FB March 2013 $21 put for $0.65 a share, or $65. Your initial investment would then be $2,700 plus the cost of the option, for a total of $2,765 (again ignoring fees and commissions).

As the price of Facebook shares drops, the price of the put option you've purchased goes up, helping offset the loss you would otherwise be incurring. If shares of Facebook rise, the value of the put option generally drops.

Also place trael stop w/ stockprices ↗ gig ? ?

If Facebook is trading *above $21* on March 15, 2013, when the put option in this example expires, you lose the $65 and you'll have to buy another put option to "protect" your investment further – which means your cost basis goes up again.

However, if Facebook is trading *below $21* on March 15, 2013, the option goes "in the money" and helps limit your loss to the difference between your purchase price of $27 and the strike price of the put option which, in this case, is $21 (again excluding fees and commissions).

Your loss is thus strictly limited to $600, plus the $65 cost of the put – even if Facebook stock plummets to, say, $15 a share.

e) Set Profit Targets

Technically, this segment should have gone up above with the other strategies for managing your winners... but I wanted to save the best for last.

It's setting simple profit targets – profits, of course, being our ultimate goal with any investment.

I'm a big fan of profit targets because they offer an unemotional path out of the market and ensure discipline, no matter how emotionally attached I become to a particular investment.

Unlike many investors, who constantly shoot for the moon, I don't see the need to be greedy. Depending on my expectations and market outlook, I'll set realistic profit targets.

They can vary widely. For conservative choices, 10% over a few months might be good. For more aggressive positions, banking more than 100% in only a few weeks – or even days – may be appropriate.

Either way, if and when a recommendation hits my price target, I'll suggest selling – with no questions asked – and bank the gains. I almost never look back.

Many investors like to think they'll do this but, in reality, they find they get sucked into the excitement of the moment. They focus on the limited potential of additional upside instead of the very real need to manage the risks associated with staying in the game longer than they ought to.

You might think this is no big deal, but I beg to differ.

Any time you attempt to second-guess the markets, you are, in effect, introducing a timing element into your decision-making process – and that's one of the most costly errors you can make.

As I have frequently noted in my speaking engagements around the globe, trying to time the markets is an exceptionally bad idea. In fact, according to studies reported in *Barron's*, the timing on 85% of all buy/sell decisions is incorrect.

Further, the latest Quantitative Analysis of Investor Behavior (QAIB) from financial services market research firm DALBAR Inc. shows that the return of an average investor trying to time the market is a pathetic 1.9% per year versus the S&P 500's return of 8.4% over the same period.

Over 20 years, that's the financial equivalent of taking a 342% hit in lost performance.

Ouch.

Putting the Method into Action

Now that you've seen and understand the five key elements of the Money Map Method – as well as the relative merits of the value-based risk minimization approach on which it's based – I want to expand a bit by detailing the actual steps I take in decided whether to buy or sell any particular asset, and when.

I divide my activities into "segmented" checklists involving the specific choices related to:

- **Existing investments** – This is the stuff I already have in play in accordance with my overall goals and objectives. (You do have goals and objectives, don't you?)

- **New investments** – This is the stuff I want to consider buying when putting new money to work.

- **Managing investments** – This is the effort devoted to managing my winners while protecting my capital against catastrophic loss.

There's obviously some overlap here, but it's all valuable information.

Evaluating Your Existing Investments

For starters, always consider your existing investments relative to the general market conditions.

What's the overall tenor of the marketplace? Is it good or bad? Are prices moving up or down?

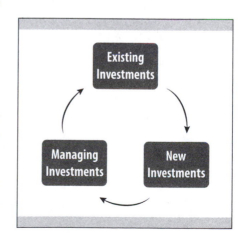

59

To make these determinations, I typically employ a proprietary version of the Coppock Indicator. This is a long-term technical tool devised by Trendex Research founder E.S.C. Coppock and first published in 1962. It was originally meant primarily to identify the start of extended bullish trends, but it can also help detect potential downturns or flat periods.

With the help of the Coppock, I decide that *it's time to reduce exposure to risk* when:

1. The economy has been strong for an extended period of time and the markets have run accordingly;

2. Stocks are expensive;

3. Initial public offering (IPO) activity is high;

4. Investors are flush and optimistic;

5. The Fed is tightening monetary policy while increasing interest rates;

6. The Coppock is above zero and falling, even as stocks continue to rise.

And, as a rule, I decide *it's time to take on added risk* when:

1. Business activity has been poor and stocks have endured a prolonged period of decline;

2. Investors have lost a lot of money and are feeling poor;

3. They're angry at Wall Street;

4. They're scared of their own shadows;

5. The Fed is lowering interest rates or engaging in other stimulative policies;

6. There's significant cash on the sidelines;

7. Ideally, the Coppock Indicator will be below zero and rising.

(**Note:** Under either set of conditions, my goal in using the Coppock is NOT to time the market, but rather to better understand the relative strength of its movements so that I know whether conditions – generally speaking – favor buying or selling.)

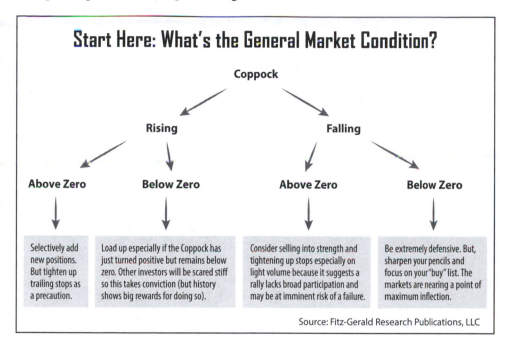

Start Here: What's the General Market Condition?

Coppock

Rising   **Falling**

Above Zero   **Below Zero**   **Above Zero**   **Below Zero**

Selectively add new positions. But tighten up trailing stops as a precaution.	Load up especially if the Coppock has just turned positive but remains below zero. Other investors will be scared stiff so this takes conviction (but history shows big rewards for doing so).	Consider selling into strength and tightening up stops especially on light volume because it suggests a rally lacks broad participation and may be at imminent risk of a failure.	Be extremely defensive. But, sharpen your pencils and focus on your "buy" list. The markets are nearing a point of maximum inflection.

Source: Fitz-Gerald Research Publications, LLC

Is a Crash Likely?

Before I act on the second set of conditions – i.e., before taking on more equity risk – I also examine the likelihood of a potential market crash.

My favorite indicator here is VERY effective – and aptly named. It's called the Hindenburg Omen, after the 1937 crash of the German Zeppelin *Hindenburg*.

Although created by an analyst named Jim Miekka, my version of the Omen, which is also proprietary, is largely based on Norman G. Fosback's High Low Logic Index (HLLI). The HLLI is the lesser of the NYSE new highs or new lows, divided by the number of NYSE issues traded, smoothed by an exponential moving average.

When the Omen signals a possible crash, it doesn't mean prices will plummet tomorrow. But it does indicate that a sharp pullback is likely within the next 30 days.

Thus, if an Omen signal has been triggered, I'll wait before initiating new long positions.

However, if there's no confirmation of the Omen reading, I'll proceed.

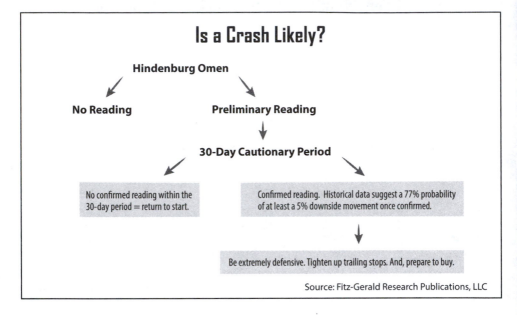

Is a Crash Likely?

Hindenburg Omen

No Reading   **Preliminary Reading**

30-Day Cautionary Period

No confirmed reading within the 30-day period = return to start.

Confirmed reading. Historical data suggest a 77% probability of at least a 5% downside movement once confirmed.

Be extremely defensive. Tighten up trailing stops. And, prepare to buy.

Source: Fitz-Gerald Research Publications, LLC

Should I Rebalance?

The other key step in deciding whether to add new investments or sell some to reduce my risk exposure involves reviewing the current allocation of assets within my basic 50-40-10 structure.

In other words, do I need to rebalance my existing mix of positions?

The review to determine whether rebalancing is needed can be time based (e.g., every three months) or dictated by certain price triggers – for example, if an existing asset or asset class rises or falls in value by 20% from its original 50-40-10 allocation. Many investors use their birthday as a reminder to review.

If prices changes have resulted in my being "over-weighted" on a particular investment or asset class, I'll usually try to sell some of those holdings and bank my profits – or, ideally, use those proceeds to buy more of the assets on which I've become "under-weighted."

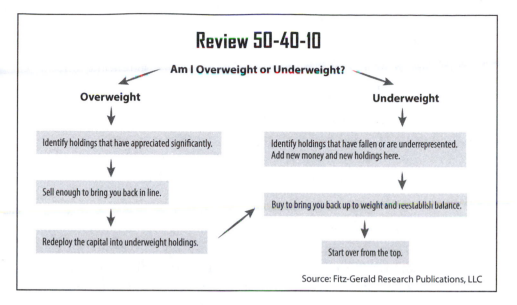

Source: Fitz-Gerald Research Publications, LLC

Then, once I've rebalanced accordingly, I'll decide how I want to put my new money to work. I base these choices not only on the merits of the individual asset, but also on maintaining the proper asset balance and risk exposure within the entire 50-40-10 portfolio.

Putting New Money to Work

As I noted earlier, I never feel compelled to buy something just because I have money available. Sometimes cash is the best thing you can hold.

However, I do believe that the markets have an inherently upward bias over time. So I look to position my new money at times when conditions favor upside activity.

Specifically, as I did above when reviewing existing holdings, I try to identify times when:

- Stocks have been in a prolonged period of decline or bouncing along a bottom

- Overall business activity has been weak

- Investors are discouraged with Wall Street and unhappy with their own equity holdings

- The Federal Reserve is moving to stimulate the economy policy and short-term interest rates are dropping

- Fund managers and investment pros are holding significant cash on the sidelines

Once I've identified a period when all (or at least a majority) of those factors are in place, I go looking for specific stocks or other assets in which to invest. As discussed in the last section, I'm looking for issues that are deeply undervalued relative to their true worth and that offer a sizable margin of safety.

To that end, you can either evaluate issues based on the Graham, Piotroski, or Negative Enterprise Value formulae outlined earlier. Or you can take the easy approach and set up a computerized screen using any of the online screening tools available today. If you choose the latter approach, I recommend basing your screens on the following parameters:

Classic Screen:
Revenue Growth YTD
         vs. year-ago YTD: ≥20%
EPS Growth Rate YOY: ≥20%
Recent Quarter Surprise: ≥5%
Annual EPS Growth: ≥20%
Next Year Growth Rate: ≥0%
Current PEG: ≤1

Deep Value Screen:
PE: <15 (and below company peers)
PEG: <1
P/B: <3 (and below company peers)
ROE: >10 (and above company peers)
EPS growth rate next five years: >5%
EPS growth rate past five years: >5%
Yield: >3%
Beta: <1

Once the screening process has given you a list of potential purchase candidates, you're still not quite done – or, at least, I'm not. Before I finally put my money into any new stock, there are several other specific things I also want to know, including:

- Can I say what the company does in one sentence?

- Do I truly understand its business?

- Is their product something the world needs, or merely wants?

- Is the company in a sector that's attracting capital or fleeing risk?

- Is the business defensible in terms of future global political and social mores?

- Does it have exposure to growing markets?

- How much free cash flow? Is it growing or shrinking? Where is it being invested?

- How much insider ownership is there?

- Are the management incentives sufficient to keep quality people without being excessive?

- Does the company have a history of using excess cash for share buybacks?

- Does it have high exposure to environmental uncertainty?

- Are there any pending legal problems?

- How much debt is the company carrying and what's the structure of that debt?

Recapping The Money Map Method at Work

In summary, then, these are the steps I take when making new investments based on the Money Map Method, and which I also consider regularly in the process of keeping *The Money Map Report* model portfolio balanced and controlling exposure to the risk of catastrophic loss:

1. Start with a review of existing holdings and how they currently fit into the 50-40-10 Strategy.

2. Screen for the best choices available, depending on which portfolio segment is ready for investment. When the markets are shaky, I place special priority on what the world *needs* as opposed to what it merely wants. Energy is an especially good example right now, as are medicine and certain types of technology. I also prefer quality companies that are in the doghouse. The deeper the value, the bigger the potential upside.

3. Prioritize results by the amount of income kicked off and the "beta" – how volatile the stock is compared to the wider market. Higher income and lower beta are best. I want to make money every day with everything in which I invest, so I deliberately look for companies

that pay me for the risk I'm taking, while also demonstrating low historical volatility.

4. Immediately put trailing stops into place. Almost without exception, I start with a figure that's 25% below my purchase price. Then, as a holding begins to climb, I ratchet the stop up in lock step. If the stock moves up by 20%, I immediately bump my trailing stop up to "entry + 5%." That way, I'm able to harvest at least a small gain, even if things go totally in the tank.

One More Strategy – How to Profit When All Else Fails

Earlier, I made the promise that, with the Money Map Method, you can still win even if the markets are terrible and it seems like the deck is stacked totally against you.

The reason that's true is because – though the vast majority of investors never take advantage of the fact – you don't have to be long to make a profit.

If you can't find anything worth buying and cash offers little or no return (as is the case now), you can almost certainly find something worth playing from the "short side."

You've already seen how buying put options can produce gains when prices for the underlying stocks or indexes fall. There are now a wide variety of exchange-traded funds (ETFs) designed to go up in value when the market or specific sectors drop – in some cases, by two or three times as much.

However, the purest means of profiting from a downward move in the market or an individual stock is by selling short.

In simplest terms, when you sell a stock short, you borrow the shares from your broker, sell them at the current market price, and then hope to score a profit by buying them back at a lower price once the stock drops. At that point, you return the shares to the broker, keeping the difference as profit (minus a small margin fee).

This is a powerful strategy, especially in uncertain times like we've experienced recently, with Europe on the ropes and the U.S. economy still struggling. If you fail to take advantage of it, you potentially leave a lot of money on the table.

How much? It's impossible to say. But stories abound about legendary traders like George Soros, who reportedly made a cool $1 billion with shorts, and John Paulson, who made even more off the housing crisis.

Of course, you can't short just any old stock and expect to profit. The key is to find overvalued issues and sell them when the market turns down, leaving long investors crying in their beer. By doing that, you can stay fully invested most of the time, getting the maximum bang for your buck.

However, you don't ever want to bet against a stock solely because it's expensive, or even overvalued.

Instead, you always want to find some other compelling reason for potential failure or a lower valuation.

You also have to be careful and spread your risk – much as you would with long positions. I suggest putting no more than 2.5% of your assets in any single short position, and limiting your short exposure in any given market sector to no more than 20% of your holdings.

Still, if you exercise some caution and screen as carefully for short candidates as you do for prospective buys, selling short can turn a bear market's doom into a profit-taker's boom.

Key Questions

A fool despises good counsel, but a wise man takes it to heart.

–Confucius

You've now gotten a fairly comprehensive overview of the Money Map Method and the five key strategic elements that make it so effective in achieving the profits we all seek in building sizable wealth – enough to help us toward a comfortable retirement.

However, without fail, whenever I speak at an investment conference or conduct a seminar, listeners nod appreciatively, then hands shoot up and the questions flow:

"That sounds great, but what about right now?"

"What are stocks going to do next?"

"What about gold?"

"How much money do I need to invest in a position?"

So let me offer my views on some of the key asset classes garnering the most attention today, as well as my advice as the Chief Investment Strategist for Money Map Press.

Q: What about gold?

A: I believe holding gold is no longer optional. Every investor needs to own it, simply because the world's central bankers have engaged in a well-intentioned, but completely irresponsible program of printing money. By its very definition, doing so is inflationary and, as such, will have a direct impact on the value of our investments.

But here's the trick. Despite widespread marketing propaganda to the contrary, gold has never, ever been statistically proven to be a viable inflation hedge.

However, it IS a fantastic crisis hedge.

Studies have shown that there is a roughly 10-to-1 inverse correlation between gold and interest rates. This suggests that investors who want to hedge the income associated with their bonds will want to own roughly $100 worth of gold for every $1,000 worth of bonds.

In addition, a portfolio holding both bonds and gold has a more attractive risk profile than one that holds either gold or bonds in isolation.

Q: What about bonds?

A: I know there's a lot of concern about a bond market crash. There has been for years.

As long as the world's central governments continue to meddle with interest rates for the wrong reasons, rates will remain low and there will be pricing support. Of course, income will stink – but that's the card we've been dealt.

As for how you handle that going forward, here's what to do: Bonds remain an important part of any investor's portfolio. And the geographic

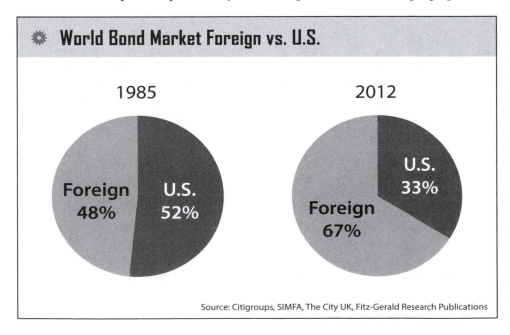

World Bond Market Foreign vs. U.S.

1985
Foreign 48%
U.S. 52%

2012
U.S. 33%
Foreign 67%

Source: Citigroups, SIMFA, The City UK, Fitz-Gerald Research Publications

shift that I described at the beginning of this book applies to global government paper, as well.

U.S. bonds, for example, accounted for 52% of the world bond market as recently as 1985. Now that figure is closer to 33% – perhaps even a bit lower. Therefore, owning foreign bonds should be an important part of the mix. If you don't, you're ignoring 67% of the potential.

Generally speaking, bonds with durations of five years or less are currently better than those with longer durations. This will help you avoid the lion's share of volatility that will inevitably come when rates finally rise – and they will. Probably sooner than most people think.

That said, I believe bonds will play out for just a bit longer. When this crisis started, I predicted yields would drop all the way to 1.5% on the 10-year note. With President Obama in office until 2016, I think we could see yields drop all the way to 1%.

As hard as it is to believe, this means there is still additional upside in bonds.

Obviously, this is going to be challenging in its own right, given that interest rates are still flirting with the extreme low end of the spectrum.

Don't forget municipal bonds, either. The same duration concept applies here: keep things short. Every state in the union has budgetary problems, and I think we're going to see a well-intentioned, but ultimately flawed national-level policy response no later than 24 months from now as many states begin to run out of money.

Q: What about real estate?

A: Real estate has no place in an average investment portfolio. Home ownership is an excuse to keep you out of the rental markets and nothing more.

You can see that very clearly in the Case-Shiller Index created by Yale economist Robert Shiller. Dating all the way back to 1890, the Index reflects the sale prices of existing houses rather than the cost of new construction so as to more cleanly track the investment value of housing over time.

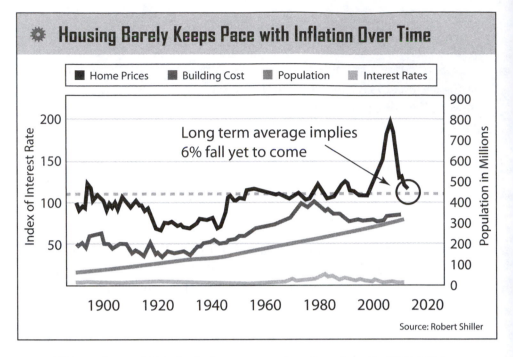

☼ **Housing Barely Keeps Pace with Inflation Over Time**

■ Home Prices   ■ Building Cost   ■ Population   ■ Interest Rates

Long term average implies
6% fall yet to come

Index of Interest Rate

Population in Millions

Source: Robert Shiller

Using a base of 100, the Index suggests that the value of a $100,000 home (adjusted for inflation in today's dollars) purchased in 1890 would sell for only $119,000 today, 122 years later. That's a mere 0.15%-a-year appreciation.

Worse, the data also suggests that prices have yet to fully revert to their average, which is 112.9263, versus the most recent index reading of 119.9263.

Put another way, existing home values have to fall another 6.0% before our nation comes into line with historical averages.

The other thing that's apparent if you look at Shiller's data is that housing prices return to their mean over time, irrespective of changes in both building costs and population – both of which are frequently cited as key real estate investment drivers.

No doubt I am going to catch lots of flak for this from real estate professionals. And I hear you guys... but hear me, too.

I am not saying real estate is always a bad investment. In fact, real estate can become significantly more valuable when its use changes and its economic density increase. For example, single-family homes are more economically dense than wheat fields. High-rises have a higher economic density than single homes. And so on.

What Ben Bernanke doesn't understand, or hasn't factored into his thinking, is that there is room for only so much economically dense property in this country. Zero interest rates or not, if you strip out the debt that allows developers to construct projects that otherwise wouldn't exist, the cash-on-cash return for housing is about what inflation offers over time.

Q: But I really want to own a house. Where do I buy?

A: In states that are not completely trashed from a fiscal standpoint. I define a "non-trashed" state as one that is not facing a disproportionately high burden from government payrolls, unfunded pension liabilities, and their own version of a welfare cliff.

California, for example, is the poster child for out-of-control spending, taxation, and welfare, followed closely by New York and Illinois. Private-sector workers are outnumbered by those on the government dole and, therefore, are more likely to get clipped if the state breaks down.

On the other hand, North Dakota, Wyoming, and Texas seem to have adult supervision. Conning & Co., a global asset manager, put together a helpful white paper titled "Municipal Credit Research – State of the States Report," in October 2012 that ranks the best to the worst.

But know that the situation remains very fluid as of this writing. Long story short, don't buy real estate in badly ill states.

Q: Should I "cherry pick" investments that sound attractive to me?

A: I know the temptation is there. I hear it all the time from *Money Map Report* subscribers who have a finely tuned radar for such "signals" as "I heard it from Uncle Bernie," "I saw it on XYZ Network," or "I got a hot tip from my nephew, who works at PDQ Technologies."

But I wouldn't.

Fad investing and overweighting takes you beyond the 50-40-10 model and significantly diminishes the risk-parity protection that's there by design.

Q: Where do small-cap stocks fit in?

A: There's no question I prefer the large, "glocal" companies at the moment. That's because they're characterized by internationally recognizable brands, have fortress-like balance sheets, and have long histories of regularly raising dividends, which means they fit perfectly within the 50-40-10 risk-parity model the Money Map Method follows.

This isn't to say there's no place for small-cap stocks in your portfolio. There is. Especially if you can identify a specific catalyst for future profitability – something like a patent or innovative proprietary game-changing technology.

My favorite small caps right now are players in the medical, bio, and defense technology fields. All three segments are developing techniques and products that could quite literally improve the lives of millions of people – and also produce some outrageous returns.

Just keep the risks in line with the rewards. That's the part too many investors forget.

Q: Do I always need to own stocks in order to make money?

A: Technically, no. With the Money Map Method, you can still win even if the markets are terrible and it seems like the deck is stacked totally against you. The reason that's true is because you don't have to be long to make a profit.

Often enough, you may not be able to find anything worth buying. Cash offers little or no return, and with inflation taking hold, keeping your money in cash can be a losing proposition.

When that happens, you can almost certainly find something worth playing from the "short side."

You've already seen how buying put options can produce gains when prices for the underlying stocks or indexes fall, and there are now a wide variety of "inverse" exchange-traded funds (ETFs) designed to go up in value when the market or specific sectors drop – in some cases, by two or three times as much.

However, the purest means of profiting from a downward move in the market or an individual stock is by selling short (which we covered on pages 66-67).

Q: Are there any specific investments or asset classes I should avoid, no matter what?

A: A key feature of the Money Map Method is that the return OF your money must be more important than the return ON your money. Period! Thus, every investment has to be made not just based on potential, but also with safety and the preservation of value in mind.

To me, this means you should:

1. Shift your focus from what the world wants to what the world needs, particularly when it comes to energy. **Luxury products and "fad investments"** should be avoided, with money instead dedicated to inflation-resistant choices and dividend-producing stocks with high free-cash flow.

2. Run, don't walk, away from **long-term bonds and fixed-rate investments**. I know this advice will irritate lots of people, but at this point that does include many annuity and whole-life insurance products. Any rise in interest rates will crater the value of these instruments and subject your wealth to unnecessary volatility.

3. Watch out for **secret "index" funds**, which claim to have special mandates or investment expertise, but really just wind up tracking the S&P 500 – with much higher costs and fees.

4. **Certificates of Deposit** (CDs), even those with five-year maturities, offer interest barely above 0%. So if you buy one, you'll virtually guarantee you're going to lose money to inflation.

Q: How much money do I need to invest using the Method?

A: It doesn't matter whether you have $10,000 to your name or $10 million. The principles are the same!

Build your pyramid from the bottom up. That way, the bulk of your money is immediately concentrated in those investments with the strongest risk-reduction characteristics. When you've got that tier covered, consider working your way "up" into global growth and income choices. Consider adding the 10% at the very top only when you've got the bulk of your assets squared away.

Q: How often do I rebalance?

A: That varies, depending on your background. Again, many investors find rebalancing annually on their birthday works well for them. Others like to rebalance quarterly. Still more prefer to keep the portfolio in motion like we do at *The Money Map Report*, making subtle adjustments monthly to reflect market conditions.

Q: What happens if...?

A: The continuing results of the global financial meltdown are scary, but they're not insurmountable. Nor inescapable.

You can still make good money and you can still protect what you've earned. In fact, it's possible to adjust the way you think about money and how you invest it to neutralize the worst of the meltdown's effects.

Remember, though, that just reading this book doesn't count. It may make you feel better. It may make you angry. It may make you any number of other things.

But you can only start down the road to financial prosperity by taking action.

Today. ***Right now!***

Conclusion

As an investor in today's markets, there is no doubt you have unique needs – from protecting what you have to growing it and building the financial legacy you want. Whether you're just starting out, about to retire, or in your golden years, the Money Map Method offers a simple, no-nonsense approach that's intended to help you save more, invest better, and build real wealth in the years ahead.

I hope the Money Map Method becomes a valuable resource for you in your financial journey now... and for years to come.

Says Who?

Opinions are like belly buttons ... everybody has one. That's why I want to back up my assertions with data and sources. Here are some of my favorite resources, with links in many instances, just in case you want to do the legwork yourself.

OECD Growth Assumptions:

The OECD models are always controversial, but my experience is that they are pretty darn well researched. Here is the full list of the OECD's growth assumptions:

A Global Vision of Long-Term Growth

	Average growth in GDP 1995-2011	Average growth in GDP 2011-2030	Average growth in GDP 2030-2060	Average growth in GDP 2011-2060	Average growth in GDP per capita 1995-2011	Average growth in GDP per capita 2011-2030	Average growth in GDP per capita 2030-2060	Average growth in GDP per capita 2011-2060
Australia	3.3	3.1	2.2	2.6	1.9	2	1.7	1.8
Austria	2	1.5	1.4	1.4	1.7	1.2	1.4	1.3
Belgium	1.8	2.1	2	2	1.3	1.5	1.7	1.6
Canada	2.6	2.1	2.3	2.2	1.6	1.3	1.8	1.6
Switzerland	1.7	2.2	2	2.1	1	1.5	1.8	1.7
Chile	3.9	4	2	2.8	2.8	3.4	2	2.5
Czech Republic	3.2	2.7	1.8	2.1	3.1	2.6	1.9	2.2
Germany	1.4	1.3	1	1.1	1.4	1.5	1.5	1.5
Denmark	1.5	1.3	2.1	1.8	1.1	1	2	1.6
Spain	2.9	2	1.4	1.7	1.9	1.6	1.3	1.4
Estonia	3.6	2.8	2	2.4	3.8	3.1	2.3	2.6
Finland	2.5	2.1	1.6	1.8	2.2	1.8	1.5	1.6
France	1.7	2	1.4	1.6	1.1	1.6	1.2	1.3
United Kingdom	2.3	1.9	2.2	2.1	1.9	1.3	1.8	1.6
Greece	2.4	1.8	1.2	1.4	1.9	1.7	1.3	1.4
Hungary	2.4	2.5	1.7	2	2.6	2.7	2	2.3
Ireland	4.7	2.1	1.7	1.9	3.2	1.3	0.9	1.1
Iceland	3	2.2	2.4	2.3	1.8	1.2	1.9	1.6
Israel	3.7	2.7	2.6	2.6	1.5	1.3	1.6	1.5
Italy	1	1.3	1.5	1.4	0.6	0.9	1.5	1.3
Japan	0.9	1.2	1.4	1.3	0.8	1.4	1.9	1.7
Korea	4.6	2.7	1	1.6	4	2.5	1.4	1.8
Luxembourg	3.8	1.8	0.6	1.1	2.3	0.7	0.1	0.3
Mexico	2.6	3.4	2.7	3	1.2	2.5	2.6	2.5
Netherlands	2.2	1.8	1.6	1.7	1.7	1.5	1.7	1.6
Norway	3	2.9	1.9	2.3	2.2	2	1.4	1.6
New Zealand	2.7	2.7	2.6	2.6	1.6	1.8	2.2	2
Poland	4.3	2.6	1	1.6	4.4	2.6	1.4	1.9
Portugal	1.7	1.4	1.4	1.4	1.3	1.4	1.6	1.5

A Global Vision of Long-Term Growth

	Average growth in GDP 1995-2011	Average growth in GDP 2011-2030	Average growth in GDP 2030-2060	Average growth in GDP 2011-2060	Average growth in GDP per capita 1995-2011	Average growth in GDP per capita 2011-2030	Average growth in GDP per capita 2030-2060	Average growth in GDP per capita 2011-2060
Slovak Republic	4.5	2.9	1.4	2	4.4	2.8	1.7	2.1
Slovenia	2.6	2	1.6	1.8	2.2	1.7	1.8	1.8
Sweden	2.5	2.4	1.8	2	2.1	1.7	1.5	1.6
Turkey	4.2	4.5	1.9	2.9	2.8	3.6	1.8	2.5
United States	2.5	2.3	2	2.1	1.5	1.5	1.5	1.5
Argentina	3.6	3.6	2.2	2.7	2.6	2.9	1.9	2.3
Brazil	3.3	4.1	2	2.8	2.1	3.4	2.1	2.6
China	10	6.6	2.3	4	9.3	6.4	2.8	4.2
Indonesia	4.4	5.3	3.4	4.1	3.1	4.5	3.3	3.8
India	7.5	6.7	4	5.1	5.8	5.6	3.6	4.4
Russia	5.1	3	1.3	1.9	5.4	3.2	1.7	2.3
Saudi Arabia	4.4	4.2	2.4	3.1	1.3	2.5	1.7	2
South Africa	3.4	3.9	2.5	3	2.1	3.4	2.3	2.7

Source: The Organization for Economic Co-operation and Development (OECD)

Selected References Related to Other Information:

- "Are Good Companies Bad Investments?," *Fortune* (February 2007)
- "How to Tell When Your Portfolio Needs a Tuneup," Smith Barney Consulting Group (2005)
- "Opportunistic Rebalancing: A New Paradigm for Wealth Managers," *Journal of Financial Planning* (January 2008)
- "The Big Picture Blog," Barry Ritholtz, www.ritholtz.com/blog/
- Advisor Perspectives, financial newsletter, advisorperspectives.com/index.php
- American Association of Individual Investors (AAII), www.aaii.com
- Bank for International Settlements, www.bis.org/
- Barron's Financial Weekly, online.barrons.com/home-page
- Benjamin Graham and David Dodd, Columbia Business School, "Security Analysis" (1934)
- Bespoke Investment Group, Financial Research and Money Management, www.bespokepremium.com
- Birinyi Associates Inc., Stock Market Research, http://www.birinyi.com/
- Burton Malkiel, "A Random Walk Down Wall Street," 10th Edition (January 2011).

- Capgemini Consulting, Global Business Perspectives, http://www.capgemini-consulting.com/
- Center For Security Research and Prices, www.crsp.com
- Country profiles, www.indexmundi.com
- Craig Mackinlay, "Multifactor Models Do Not Explain Deviations from the CAPM," *Journal of Financial Economics 69* (1995)
- Craig McCann and Dengpan Luo, "Concentrated Investments, Uncompensated Risk and Hedging Strategies," (October 19, 2004)
- Dalbar Investment Research, www.dalbar.com
- EPFR Global, Equity Fund Flows – Daily, Weekly and Monthly Data, Dec. 7, 2012 Report.
- ETF Analytics, www.indexuniverse.com
- F. Douglas Foaster, Tom M. Smith and Robert Whaley, "Assessing Goodness of Fit of Asset Pricing Models: The Distribution of R2," *Journal of Finance 52* (June 1997)
- Fisher Black, "Beta and Return," *Journal of Portfolio Management 20* (Fall 1993).
- Forbes Magazine, www.forbes.com/forbes
- G.P. Brinson, L.R. Hood, G.L. Beebower – "Determinants of Portfolio Performance" (1986)
- Harry Markowitz, University of California-San Diego, "Modern Portfolio Theory" (1959)
- International Business Times, Global Business News, www.ibtimes.com/
- James Tobin, "Liquidity Preference as Behavior Towards Risk," *Review of Economic Studies 25.1* (1958)
- Jan Mossin, Norwegian School of Economics, "Equilibrium in a Capital Asset Market," *Econometrica 34* (1966)
- Jason Zweig, "Your Money and Your Brain: How the New Science of Neuroeconomics Can Help Make You Rich," Simon & Schuster (2007)
- John Burr Williams, "The Theory of Investment Value," Harvard Business School (1938)
- John Burr Williams, "The Theory of Investment Value" (1928)
- John V. Lintner Jr., "Capital Asset Pricing Model," Harvard Business School (1965)
- Kent Womack and Ying Zhang, "Understanding Risk and Return, the CAPM and the Fama-French Three Factor Model." Tuck Case No. 03-111 (December 19, 2003)

- Louis Bachelier, "Theorie de la Speculation," *Annales Scientifique de l'École Normale Superiéure*, 3rd Series 17 (1900)
- Lu Zhang, "The Value Premium," Simon School of Business, *Working Paper No. FR -2-19* (November 13, 2002)
- MH Professional, "Why Invest for Dividends?" www.mhprofessional.com/downloads/products/0071769609/0071769609_peris_ch_1.pdf
- Ned Davis Research,www.ndr.com
- Robert Shiller, Arthur M. Okun Professor of Economics, Yale University, http://www.econ.yale.edu/~shiller
- Royal Bank of Canada, www.rbc.com/country-select.html
- U.S. Department of Labor - Bureau of Labor Statistics, http://www.bls.gov/
- William F. Sharpe, Stanford University, "Multi-Period Asset Allocation," *Journal of Portfolio Management* (Fall 1994)
- Wilshire Associates, Investment Research and Management, www.wilshire.com

Money Map Building Blocks

The Money Map Method in a Nutshell

The world, both financial and cultural, is rapidly changing. That doesn't mean we can ignore the past.

History may not repeat, but it does "rhyme," so we must frequently look back in order to truly see forward.

Sitting on the sidelines in tumultuous times such as we're seeing now may feel good, but it is the worst possible mistake investors can make. Remember, **you miss 100% of the swings you never take**.

There is more information available to investors and analysts today than ever before. You've got 24-hour business news, multiple market-oriented TV networks, instantly updating technical-analysis programs, and quote services streaming data to every laptop and notebook computer. You can even get instant market information via your mobile phones.

Sadly, much of this information turns out to be misinformation – little more than daily "noise," with a few lukewarm "hot tips" sprinkled in. One need look no further than the über-hype surrounding the run-up to Facebook's 2012 IPO for an example of investors being sold a bill of goods – and getting screwed in the process.

That's why today it's more important than ever to understand the key drivers that propel prices higher in times of optimism – and keep them there in times of fear. **Deep value will trump trendy, high-risk stocks every time and especially *over* time**.

Despite its widespread appeal to amateurs and heavy promotion by some financial pundits, **"timing" the markets is an exercise in futility**. It results in significantly worse performance over time. The risks of missing out on major bull moves due to bad timing far outweigh the potential benefits of avoiding minor market downturns.

Traditional diversification models are badly broken. **Risk-parity based concentration** is much more effective than blindly spreading your money around when it comes to controlling risk and enhancing returns.

Income plays a far more important role in total returns than most investors understand. Wall Street cannot, or will not, tell the truth about this because it is against its own best interests – i.e., trading volume is substantially lower among income investors than among those who chase growth.

The ultimate measure of retirement is having enough money to meet your goals and support the lifestyle you've always dreamed of. However, the financial crisis has created a fundamental change in the focus retirement planning must take, shifting the emphasis from pursuit of opportunistic gains to development of a lifetime income plan.

Be a "nowist," not a futurist. Capitalizing on long-term trends is a key to investment success, but it's one thing to identify rapidly emerging trends and entirely another to understand the moves you need to make ahead of time to maximize the opportunity they offer.

All investing involves risk – but not all risks are the same.

History demonstrates beyond any shadow of a doubt that the greatest gains go to those who invest when the masses are headed for the hills. For example, investors with the courage to deploy new money in stocks in March 2009 (after a quick and painful 56.77% drawdown in the S&P 500) were rewarded with a 106% return in just 36 months – and prices are even higher as I write.

Similar situations existed throughout history – most notably in 2003, in 1987, through the 1970s, and in 1954, 1929, 1891, and 1873 – with each rally immediately preceded by a material crisis and market swoon.

Remember, bear tracks always come before a running of the bulls, so **relish downturns**.

Structure – and specifically the 50-40-10 portfolio model that is the foundation of *The Money Map Method* – is much more important than individual stock selection when it comes to delivering the most favorable risk/reward ratio over the long term.

Therefore, achieving investment success is a matter of quantifying risks that generate expected returns and eliminating those that don't.

Again, in today's markets, the return OF your capital is much more crucial than the return ON your capital.

A Special Note Regarding Sources and Statistics:

Wherever possible, I have cited many of the statistics used in this book. Others are not. This is simply a function of the sheer volume of data, research, and material I encounter in my daily routine, the frequency with which it changes, and the internationalization of the underlying concepts as they move into mainstream thinking. Please also note that many figures are presented in general context only and are subject to change without warning based on market developments and geopolitical maneuvering. I would like to thank the many researchers, market professionals, and management of securities companies, brokers, government agencies, and consulting firms who supply me with up-to-the-minute information daily.

Finally, while I reference a wide variety of sources and materials, I have received no compensation for doing so. I mention them because they have been helpful to me and I hope they will be helpful to you, the readers.

About Keith Fitz-Gerald

KEITH FITZ-GERALD is an internationally recognized expert on global markets, a media contributor, and renowned futurist. Forbes named him Keith a "Business Visionary" in 2010.

In his capacity as Chief Investment Strategist for Money Map Press, he regularly appears on Fox Business Network, CNBC Asia, BNN, and more. He has been in cited in *The Wall Street Journal*, *WIRED*, and Forbes.com, among other publications.

Keith holds a B.S. in management and finance from Skidmore College and an M.S. in international finance (with a focus on Japanese business science) from Chaminade University. He splits his time between the United States and Japan with his wife and two sons, and he regularly travels the world in search of investment opportunities others don't yet see – or recognize.

About *The Money Map Report*

The Money Map Report is a leading independent source of investing information in today's complex financial markets, providing insight, analysis, and commentary backed by more than 100 years of combined, expert experience. **Keith Fitz-Gerald** serves as the Chief Investment Strategist for the *Report*, which has over 40,000 subscribers throughout North America, Europe, and Asia.